D0630077

WHAT PEOPLE ARE SAYING ABOUT
*IT'S YOUR TIME*

This work is overdue yet timely, confrontational yet comforting, philosophical yet practical, detailed yet comprehensive, challenging yet instructive, and a must for anyone who desires to understand the times and how we should respond as Kingdom Citizens in the 21st Century. I recommend this book without hesitation and suggest you also buy one for a friend.  —Dr. Myles E. Munroe
Founder and President
BFM International
Nassau, Bahamas

As a voice crying in the wilderness, Eddie Long is not afraid to speak the truth with great power and integrity. *It's Your Time* will convict and inspire you to move from a lukewarm existence to being on fire for God and His perfect plan for your life. I challenge you to read this book and try and stay the same...impossible!  —Dr. Tony Evans
Senior Pastor, Oak Cliff Bible Fellowship
President, The Urban Alternative

Bishop Eddie Long is a man of courage and commitment and has dedicated his life to changing lives and building communities of faith. *It's Your Time* will motivate every reader to move in the Spirit to do God's work for those who have been left out and left behind.  —Thomas W. Dortch, Jr.
Chairman Emeritus of 100 Black Men of America, Inc.

There must be a renewed sense of urgency amongst believers in the area of taking back all that the enemy has stolen and claiming what is rightfully our inheritance as children of God. Bishop Eddie Long's timely new release, *It's Your Time*, speaks to that urgency as he equips readers with practical weapons that we can apply right now to walk boldly with God-given authority into our destiny!
—Paula White
Paula White Ministries

I strongly recommend as mandatory reading *It's Your Time* for a troubled society. Bishop Long speaks with authority as a true visionary and man of God. Bishop has given us a mandate to follow for reclaiming what is rightfully ours. In a world where there is an overflowing and an abundance of "milk and honey" no one, especially the least of these, should be left behind. I guarantee after reading *It's Your Time* you too will witness as Paul in Philippians 2:13 *"for it is God who worketh in you both to will and to do of His good pleasure."* This is a best seller and a book that you will continue to use as a reference point when we together "reclaim what the devil has stolen."

—The Honorable Andrew Young
Chairman, GoodWorks International, LLC.
Former Mayor, City of Atlanta, Georgia,
United States Congressman from the State of Georgia &
Ambassador to the United Nations

Bishop Eddie Long is one of the inspiring and creative evangelical churchmen in America. I was blown away by the wonderful church and ministry I saw for the first time at Coretta Scott King's memorial service. Now comes the book! It captivates the heart of a great man's ministry from whom we can all learn. He is a leader with passion, purpose and principle. I thank him for his ministry and his book.

—Robert H. Schuller
Founding Pastor
Crystal Cathedral Ministries

If ever there was a voice profoundly called to the nation to make us aware of the time, that voice is Bishop Eddie L. Long. In the book, *It's Your Time,* he reminds us that even the demons are subject to the name of Jesus when that name is used by believers who are called to take authority and have dominion in the earth. To the citizens of this kingdom, this book is a must-read…it's your time!

—Bishop George G. Bloomer
Best-selling Author

# IT'S YOUR TIME

## RECLAIM YOUR TERRITORY FOR THE KINGDOM

# IT'S YOUR TIME

## RECLAIM YOUR TERRITORY FOR THE KINGDOM

# EDDIE LONG

WHITAKER
HOUSE

Unless otherwise indicated, Scripture quotations are taken from the *New King James Version*, © 1979, 1980, 1982, 1984 by Thomas Nelson, Inc. Used by permission. All rights reserved. Scripture quotations marked (NASB) are taken from the updated *New American Standard Bible®*, NASB®, © 1960, 1962, 1963, 1968, 1971, 1972, 1973, 1975, 1977, 1995 by The Lockman Foundation. Used by permission. (www.Lockman.org). Scripture quotations marked (KJV) are taken from the King James Version of the Holy Bible.

## IT'S YOUR TIME:
### RECLAIM YOUR TERRITORY FOR THE KINGDOM

New Birth Missionary Baptist Church
P.O. Box 1019
Lithonia, GA 30058
770 696 9600
www.newbirth.org

ISBN-13: 978-0-88368-783-3
ISBN-10: 0-88368-783-6
Printed in the United States of America
© 2006 by Eddie Long

1030 Hunt Valley Circle
New Kensington, PA 15068
www.whitakerhouse.com

**Library of Congress Cataloging-in-Publication Data**
Long, Eddie.
It's your time : reclaim your territory for the kingdom / Eddie Long.
p.    cm.
Summary: "A call for the church to reclaim the Kingdom inheritance that God has given her"—Provided by publisher.
ISBN-13: 978-0-88368-783-3 (trade hardcover : alk. paper)
ISBN-10: 0-88368-783-6 (trade hardcover : alk. paper)
1. Church renewal—Baptists.  I. Title.
BV600.3.L66 2006
269—dc22                2006008971

No part of this book may be reproduced or transmitted in any form or by any means, electronic or mechanical—including photocopying, recording, or by any information storage and retrieval system—without permission in writing from the publisher. Please direct your inquiries to permissionseditor@whitakerhouse.com.

3  4  5  6  7  8  9  10  11  12  ᵾ  15  14  13  12  11  10  09  08  07  06

# CONTENTS

CHAPTER 1

# TAKING IT BACK

On a blustery winter day, nearly twenty-five thousand believers sang worship songs and marched as a united army. Praying under showers of light rain, we flowed through the city streets of Atlanta like a mighty river, joined in the power of holy unity. On that day, we became one voice, a clarion call for righteousness that would not be denied.

On December 11, 2004, New Birth Missionary Baptist church organized this march through the city of Atlanta. We began at the late Reverend Martin Luther King Jr.'s gravesite and ended at Turner Field. Reverend King's daughter Bernice launched the march by lighting a torch at her father's grave and passing it on to me. I carried that torch for two miles as we advanced through the city.

Our goal: to take a stand and make a statement of our belief that marriage is between one man and one woman. Other goals included programs that create wealth for the lesser privileged, the promotion of educational reform, and affordable health care. This is not a white issue or a black issue or a brown issue. This is a human issue; a Christian issue. As God's children, we need to stand united in taking back what the enemy has stolen from us.

As one massive kingdom voice, we made a loud and bold proclamation for morality, purity, and holiness, as a people, as a country, and as a church, to a nation that has lost its way. We marched to announce our intention to take back what the devil has stolen. We will not be deterred. We will not be turned around. We will not be denied.

The godless didn't like it, and we were met with persecution and slander. We expected nothing less. Our march harkened back to a march a long time ago, when as a black people, we united and began a decades-long struggle to reclaim our human dignity and our civil rights.

> **As Christians, we must unite and reclaim what we have lost!**

Today, our mandate is no less urgent and no less vital. As a Christian people, we must unite once again and reclaim what we have lost. We're under a mandate—*a kingdom mandate*—for change. And we *will* triumph!

That is the reason I've written this book. For too long we've held back, we've kept our peace, and we've allowed the ungodly to determine our destiny as a people, as a nation, and as individuals. We are the church of the living God; we are the head and not the tail. (See Deuteronomy 28:13.) Yet, sadly, we've lain down and permitted the devil to run over us while we've lived in division, pettiness, and strife.

Yet, a new day has arrived. A day for reclaiming the kingdom promise and the purpose of our existence. With this message I herald the promise of this book: we are destined to take it back, and we're succeeding with a bold force that cannot be stopped.

If you're living beneath your full entitlement as a child of destiny, this book is for you. As God's own son or daughter, I command you to rise up and lay hold of that for which you've been created and saved. Your nation and your world need you to fully realize your position as God's son or daughter in this crucial hour. It is my prayer that these pages will undergird you with wisdom, insight, and power to rise up and to take it back!

You are not a beggar in God's kingdom, pleading for crumbs from His table. You are a king or a queen, and a priest. In order to reclaim what's yours, you will first need to change the way you've been thinking: as a kingdom son or daughter, you need to begin developing a kingdom mind-set. (See Revelation 1:6; 5:10.)

> *In God's kingdom, you are a king or a queen, and a priest.*

## Kingdom Thinking

God is calling us up higher, to a new dimension of living. He is moving us into "kingdom dimensions." Please understand that God appoints kings. That is why He is called the King of Kings, and Lord of Lords.

The body of Christ seems to greatly struggle with the fact that God raises up certain men and women to be His voice. He speaks to His own through servants whom He commissions as a voice of liberation, a voice of direction, and a voice that moves them into their destiny.

Three and a half million Israelites died in the wilderness instead of entering into the land of promise. Do you know why? It was for this very reason: twelve leaders went into the Promised Land to spy it out and bring the people back a report. But ten of those twelve leaders brought back a wrong report. These ten were the leaders of the tribes—they were not young and inexperienced. Neither were they newly saved. These ten out of twelve preached the wrong sermon, and three and a half million folk chose to follow them to a long, slow, hot death in the wilderness. God never sanctioned what these ten leaders spoke. And so they all died in the wilderness.

You may not realize it, but the trip from Egypt to the Promised Land was an eleven-day journey. Imagine how far you could travel in eleven days by walking every day and resting at night. Then consider that three and a half million people wandered around an area that small for forty years until they died in the desert! If that sounds like foolishness and madness, it was!

That same thing has been going on in the body of Christ. We have been wandering around in circles in the wilderness of our low expectations, because we don't understand and have not yet learned to walk in the ways of God's kingdom.

## Thy Kingdom Come

I want to push this a little further. Consider the simplicity of Jesus when the disciples asked Him to teach us how to pray. He taught us to pray according to this pattern: *"Our Father who art in heaven, hallowed be Thy name. Thy kingdom come. Thy will be done on earth as it is in heaven"* (Matthew 6:9–10 NASB).

Christ did not say, "Thy 'church' come..." He said, *"Thy kingdom come. Thy will be done on earth as it is in heaven."*

After addressing these matters, He went on to more personal things. *"Give us this day our daily bread. And forgive us our debts, as we also have forgiven our debtors. And do not lead us into temptation, but deliver us from evil"* (verses 11–12 NASB).

The kingdom statement was made first, and then the personal matters were dealt with as a kind of subset of the Lord's sweeping statements about His kingdom. In other words, if His kingdom does not come, neither does our daily bread.

Accordingly, without the arrival of His kingdom, no grace can be extended with which to forgive or to be forgiven. Nor is there anything to restrain us from being led into evil.

God tells us that without His kingdom we will not eat. Yet, we take this little prayer and we play with it like some toy. We consider it oh so cute—the prayer we graduated to after we mastered "Now I lay me down to sleep."

This spiritual immaturity dismisses the great weight of dynamic biblical truth. God was saying, "I've come to establish a kingdom." John the Baptist understood this bold proclamation when he preached, "Repent, for the kingdom of heaven is at hand." (See Mark 1:15.)

## TODAY'S JOSHUAS AND CALEBS

The Israelites wandered in the wilderness for forty years because they listened to the wrong voices. Still, God gave them the opportunity to hear the right ones. They were not in the majority, but their voices were heard. Had the Israelites listened to these voices, they would have enjoyed the benefits of the Promised Land right away without a generation of pain, disappointment, heartache, struggle, and death.

God has raised up voices in this hour that harken the voices of Joshua and Caleb, crying out to those who can hear. But don't look for them among the majority, for the majority cannot hear them. Only those who have been broken have the ability to hear. That is the reason why God takes us through seasons of breaking and humbling in our lives, so that we might become totally broken.

> *Only those who have been broken have the ability to hear His voice.*

Why does He need to break us? So that we can learn His voice. In this hour, more than ever, you need to be able to discern whether you are hearing from God.

I do not assume that you will hear these Joshuas and Calebs because you are listening to leaders on television. The only qualification an individual needs to get on TV is enough money to pay for the airtime. Just because someone is speaking on television does not mean they are a leader with a voice that can lead you to the Promised Land.

It's time we gained the discernment to hear the Joshuas and Calebs of our time. I don't know about you, but my heart is longing for the fullness of God's promises, and I am weary because we've been wandering in the wilderness far too long.

### TEARING DOWN THE JERICHO WALLS

I want to abolish the walls of Jericho once and for all, because I am not in the wilderness any longer! If you are reading this book, I believe you are an individual who is walking in God's promises. It's time we rip down those walls.

The walls have been fortified for a long time with the purpose of keeping God's people locked out of our promises. We've been locked out of employment, wealth, healing, and much more. There are many people who are sick because they don't have the resources to stay well.

I am here to tell you the devil is a liar. We are God's people, and we will blow down these walls and nothing will be denied to us. Everything that has been locked up in the city, everything that has been locked up in the state, and everything that has been locked up in the nation will be released into the hands of God's children through the mighty shout of the Holy Spirit.

In order to release the Holy Spirit's shout in your life, you must become a true worshipper. God will accept nothing less, but you must worship Him in spirit and in truth. This is what it will take to bless the Lord and release His mighty shout.

### RELEASING A SHOUT

You may not understand what I mean by "releasing a shout," but to pull down those walls of resistance to God's kingdom and our promises, you must. Releasing a shout is vitally important to establishing God's kingdom.

15

Let me explain. If I were to set a radio in front of you, plug in into a power source and turn it on, I'd pick up all kinds of stuff that's out there right now on the airways. But without a radio I can't pick up anything. If I don't happen to have a radio, that doesn't mean the signals are not out there. They are, but I cannot hear them because I don't have the electronic "ears" to hear. Similarly, when you lift up spiritual praise to the Lord, it doesn't go away simply because you stop hearing it. Your praise releases *virtue* into the atmosphere.

In our own city, we've had faithful men and women praying continually, worshipping God. They have filled the atmosphere with prayer and praise, just as the Israelites did when they circled Jericho during their seven-day march. But when the time was right, when God spoke a word through their leader, they released all that power with a unified shout.

We realized the power of the shout just days before the last election. When the battle raged and much hung in the balance, our people united in prayer. We released a deafening shout of praise into the atmosphere, directed toward Washington D.C., the city of Atlanta, and toward our own neighborhood of Lithonia, Georgia.

The united prayer and praise of God's people releases great power. His kingdom comes through His people. My congregation conducts prayer meetings on a regular basis. I told them that when we unite in prayer to raise a "shout," they'd know the leaders of this country were sovereignly ordained. This event took place before the last election when the entire country was locked in fierce political conflict over who would lay the foundation of national leadership to lead our nation into the new millennium.

God had spoken to me earlier, and He told me to unite my people in prayer and worship and to release a "shout" into the atmosphere. God would unite our prayers with the prayers of others around the country to set into position a God-serving leader. After the shout, we would know that God had already chosen His leaders, and the current and future presidents would know that God is in charge of this nation.

When God can find people who are submitted to leadership, those with one voice, whose united vision is to see the kingdom come and God's perfect will be done in His perfect timing, He can then release His power. If our shout hooks up with *God has already chosen His leaders, and God is in charge of this nation.* the heart cry of other believers, our voices will be directed like a laser beam into the spiritual realm.

There will be believers who have the key to the back door of the White House. Others will walk onto the floor of the Senate and House, slam down a Bible, and declare the word of the Lord. They will proclaim that certain activities and behaviors will end, and godliness shall begin.

## Taking It Back

Do you believe in the miraculous power of God? Do you believe that what God has promised to His people is in our hands? That every place that the sole of your foot shall tread is already yours? (See Joshua 1:3). If so, then rise up and take authority. Unite your voice with others and boldly assert your power as a believer.

We at New Birth united in one bold, spiritual force and declared to the kingdom of darkness: *We claim our young people back! We claim our children back! We declare that our families are coming back to God! We declare the wealth of the wicked belongs to the righteous! We demand that all the devil has stolen come back to us right now!*

Now is the time for the saints of the Most High God to rise up and possess the kingdom. Are you a believer, or a doubter? Choose to rise up in faith, not wavering. Now is your time to kick in the gates of hell and gain access as never before.

God needs people who can handle power and authority. God needs folks He can trust. Can He trust you with money? Can He trust you with creative ideas that will rock cities and stir nations? Can He trust you to seek and follow His will for your life?

When the Israelites circled Jericho, they were seeking access. The blessings of God were locked away from them behind mighty walls that seemed impossible to penetrate. The blessings God had promised them were held by their ene-mies—the residents of Jericho who opposed them. In order to realize the blessings of God in their lives, in order to take back what God had already given them, they needed to get behind those walls. They needed access.

When the Israelites sized up the insurmountable walls, they prayed and God told them to release a shout. His ways are not our ways. We attempt to tear down the walls erected against our promise and purpose through man-made programs. But

God doesn't need our programs and strategies. Are you ready to leave your program and get on God's program?

God says, "I am looking for believers. I am looking for the redeemed of the Lord so I can pronounce a blessing over you." If that is you, I proclaim His blessing upon you and may it rest upon you mightily. This is the blessing I declare upon you at this very moment: Access, access, access, access! In the name of Jesus, the doors of opportunity and blessing are opened to your life through the power of His mighty name.

God says, "While you were praying for others, I was overseeing your concerns. While you were praying for the release in your nation, I was releasing you in this nation."

When Joshua released the people's shout, it was directed toward the walls with one united voice and vision. Every one of those soldiers had a unique need, but everything they needed was on the other side of those walls. Individually, they couldn't be selfish and talk about what they needed person-

> *The doors of blessing are opened through the power of His name.*

ally. If all were not blessed together, then none would be blessed alone. In order to find the kingdom, they had to realize there was a leader whom God had raised up to go before them. Joshua, their leader, was no wimp. He boldly heard and followed the word of the Lord.

## GOD'S CHOSEN LEADERS

We love hearing the stories of leaders such as Moses, Elijah, and Paul because they are dead. We love to study and shout about them. If they were alive today, few of us would follow them. Why? Because following a great leader exacts a great price from us—one that few are willing to pay.

The modern church's view and understanding of its leadership has wreaked havoc in the body of Christ and perpetrated much damage. Few believers in our generation understand and accept that God places vision and a corporate destiny in the hearts of men and women. He fully intends that the sheep submit to such leaders. Just because a few leaders have been exposed as frauds does not suggest that God has changed the way He works in the church. He fully intends that we receive Him through the gifts, vision, and anointing He has bestowed upon various leaders. They are worthy of our respect, not because of who they are in the flesh, but because God has chosen them and set them in place.

## Praying in the "Already"

One final matter is vitally important for releasing a shout that will cause the walls of resistance in your life to crumble. In order to release a shout, you must change your prayer language. Let me explain. You'll recall that God finished everything at the beginning of time. If you read Genesis, you'll find that everything was finished. When He completed His plan, He then began the generations of Adam.

It's vitally important to understand that God did not send us to do the work of mankind. He sent us *because* it was already done. He completed His plan for mankind, and then He went back and started our history. He didn't send us to do it; He sent us because it was already done. That's why He tells us that *"every place that the sole of your foot will tread upon I **have given** you"* (Joshua 1:3, emphasis added). That means that every place the soles of your foot tread upon has *already* been given to you. Therefore, when you pray you must pray in the "already." God does not send you to accomplish His purpose—He has already done so! He sends you to enforce what He has already completed.

### Reclaiming Our Young

I have "the already" in my spirit. In order to release a shout, you too must stand in the now and pray in the "already," with full conviction that God is hearing and moving at the exact moment you're calling to Him.

Let me explain what I mean. Praying in the "already" means you are expecting an answer not in a few days, not by next year, but in the very moment you pray. The act of praying is actually moving the matter, the problem, or the issue. You come to God knowing the answer has "already" been given, and your prayer is an act of receiving the answer in the here and now. When Joshua and the Israelites lifted up a shout, the walls came tumbling down *while they were still shouting.* That's what it means to pray in the "already."

If you pray "process" prayers, then you get an answer in a month or a year—you can actually put your answer on hold by praying that way. Process prayers are those prayed hoping that sometime in the future they will be heard and answered. Recently, when I began praying with my congregation, declaring that our young people would return to the Lord, our people spontaneously broke out in praises and a shout, even though the young people were not in the sanctuary. At that very moment, many of our teenagers were stopped in their tracks by the Spirit of God. Literally in that same hour, they began pouring into the sanctuary.

We pray "mega" prayers, which is a term we've coined to suggest the amazing, instantaneous release of prayer power to work God's purposes and plans. A "mega" prayer means *it is finished, I declare it, it is done right now.*

Let's declare a "mega" prayer over your life right now: You are walking in power, authority, healing, and prosperity. Your soul is prospering and you have dominion. You have dominion over the state in which you live, and over the city into which you've been placed by the Almighty God.

> **We are the church of Jesus Christ, and this is our finest hour!**

This is our nation and our world. We are the church of Jesus Christ, and this is our finest hour!

## Raising Our Shout in the Streets of Atlanta

Our march through Atlanta that blustery day was a demonstration of unity and dominion by God's people. It was not without conflict. We marched under a haze of ugly and often nasty propaganda from gay and lesbian groups and the press. But the opposition of the pitifully few was barely audible next to the magnificent shout made by the massive assembly of the righteous men and women marching on the side of the Lord.

The future of this nation does not rest in the hands of politicians. Our future is held by godly people from the east to the west coast who will rise up and lift their voices on behalf of godliness. It is time to take to the streets and declare: "Enough is enough! We are unwilling to remain silent while the sanctity of marriage and the family is being attacked."

Daniel 4:3 says, *"His kingdom is an everlasting kingdom."* You can have an everlasting kingdom without power, but the verse doesn't stop there. It says, *"And His dominion is from generation to generation."* God has an everlasting kingdom, but His dominion—His supremacy, His authority—is from generation to generation. Therefore, we marched united with those bold prophets of the past, our fathers and mothers who stood up to be counted. And we marched with our children holding our hands and our babies in our arms. Our generations are built upon a firm foundation of righteousness, a solid rock of truth.

We marched in the streets to declare Christ's dominion over the homosexual agenda and over principalities and powers that work to rob and diminish the power of God's people. God's children are rising up in this dark hour to take back what the devil has stolen. We lifted up a shout, a bold declaration before the entire nation that the kingdom of God has come and God's will *will* be done! We will not be silenced, we will not be defeated, we shall not be moved.

CHAPTER 2

# A KINGDOM MANDATE

The entire nation gasped in shock and disbelief as the early reports trickled in. A tsunami of unprecedented proportions washed entire towns, villages, and people out to sea. Without warning, an underground earthquake created waves believed to be as high as one hundred feet, traveling to shore from four hundred to six hundred miles per hour. The early death toll reports were incomprehensible. In the end, more than one hundred fifty thousand from several Asian nations were swept to their deaths.

What happened? The earth shifted. There was a realignment of the foundations upon which the earth rested.

I want to provide prophetic insight to this event and so many others that have occurred very recently. The tsunami came at the end of a hurricane season recorded as one of the worst in history. Nine hurricanes cost American taxpayers forty-two billion dollars in damages.

Prophetically, I believe we have entered a time of spiritual alignments and kingdom adjustments. Great earthquakes and mighty shakings are happening in the spiritual realm. The physical realm is merely reflecting this spiritual reality.

How is the body of Christ connected to all of these events? Is God involved in this unprecedented time in which we're living? In order to advance in the kingdom business of the Father, you must be well equipped with a good understanding and spiritual insight into these dramatic and often tragic times we live in.

## TRYING CIRCUMSTANCES

When John the Baptist was locked up, he seemed perplexed that Jesus—the One he was announcing—did not come to the jail to break him out or at least to visit. Seemingly filled with confusion and doubt, John asked a loaded question. *"Are You the Coming One, or do we look for another?"* (Matthew 11:3). In other words, was Jesus really the Christ? John had prepared the way and preached that Jesus had come, but sitting in the dark cell awaiting execution seemed to have played tricks on his brain.

Jesus answered his question, *"Blessed is he who is not offended because of Me"* (Matthew 11:6).

There will be some people that will get caught up in concerns that God never addresses. They seem to think God should be sweating over what's bothering them, but He's not. They are deeply concerned, and in their eyes He seems not to care. It can make such an individual very upset with God. That's why Jesus said, "Blessed are those who don't get upset with the things that I do."

## SIGNS OF OUR TIMES

There is no way to possibly explain or try to figure out everything. The earthquake that has devastated lives and

26

people must be understood and addressed in order to provide clarity. Nevertheless, the things I'm about to say are meat, not milk. They are easily misunderstood; and as most of us know, misunderstandings often bring offense. Pray and ask God to give you ears to hear what the Spirit of God is saying.

> *So they asked Him, saying, "Teacher, but when will these things be? And what sign will there be when these things are about to take place?"...And there will be signs in the sun, in the moon, and in the stars; and on the earth distress of nations, with perplexity, the sea and the waves roaring; men's hearts failing them from fear and the expectation of those things which are coming on the earth, for the powers of the heavens will be shaken. Then they will see the Son of Man coming in a cloud with power and great glory. Now when these things begin to happen, look up and lift up your heads, because your redemption draws near.*
>
> (Luke 21:7, 25–28)

When these things begin to happen, the Lord tells us to "look up, for your redemption draws near." These are the signs of the time in which we live.

When God speaks of the sun, moon, and stars, He is telling us that the order of alignment in this universe will be impacted during this hour of time. When we look at matters of alignment, we must understand that God has ordained an order in the universe: first the natural and then the spiritual.

It's vitally important when we begin to walk in newness of life in the Holy Spirit that we walk in those things He has ordained for us. We must walk in righteousness by becoming the fully functioning body of Jesus Christ. In order to do so, we each must find our individual part in His body and walk therein. We must quit trying to be someone else, and stop walking in jealousy, envy, and strife. Your place in the body is as important as anyone else's place, because every divine assignment is essential.

> *Every divine assignment is essential to the body of Christ.*

We see the sun, moon and stars mentioned again in the twelfth chapter of Revelation:

> *Now a great sign appeared in heaven: a woman clothed with the sun, with the moon under her feet, and on her head a garland of twelve stars. Then being with child, she cried out in labor and in pain to give birth. And another sign appeared in heaven: behold, a great, fiery red dragon having seven heads and ten horns, and seven diadems on his heads. His tail drew a third of the stars of heaven and threw them to the earth. And the dragon stood before the woman who was ready to give birth, to devour her Child as soon as it was born. She bore a male Child who was to rule all nations with a rod of iron. And her Child was caught up to God and His throne. Then the woman fled into the wilderness, where she has a place prepared by God, that they should feed her there one thousand two hundred and sixty days.*
>
> (Revelation 12:1–6)

The woman is a symbol of the church of Jesus Christ, and she is in pain to birth God's rulership in the earth. Christ taught that the sun, moon, and stars would be signs of the end of the age; and here in the apocalyptic book of Revelation we see those signs.

### THE SYMBOL OF THE SUN

The sun is a symbol representing Jesus Christ, for it is a revelation of Him. He is bringing forth revelation in this hour that is bigger than ever—it's global. When we speak of the sun, we understand that the light of revelation from the Spirit of God has been granted.

The apostle Peter received revelation from God regarding the true identity of Christ. Jesus said, "Who do you say that I am?"

> *He saith unto them, But whom say ye that I am? And Simon Peter answered and said, Thou art the Christ, the Son of the living God. And Jesus answered and said unto him, Blessed art thou, Simon Barjona: for flesh and blood hath not revealed it unto thee, but my Father which is in heaven. And I say also unto thee, That thou art Peter, and upon this rock I will build my church; and the gates of hell shall not prevail against it.* (Matthew 16:15–18 KJV)

### THE SYMBOL OF THE MOON

In the passage from Revelation 12, the Lord also referred to signs involving the moon. The moon reflects the glory of the sun in the darkness of the night. As such, the moon is also a symbol of the church, for it reflects the light of Christ into the darkness of the world. The church must be in proper alignment with the Son in order to reflect His glory.

29

When God reveals himself, He is *light* and the source of all light, just as the sun illuminates the earth. The moon has no light of its own, for it cannot reflect light unless it exists in proper alignment to the sun.

The moon must come into alignment with the sun: first the sun, then the moon. The moon shines brightest when it is in perfect alignment with the sun. And the light within the church shines brightest when it is in perfect alignment, or relationship, to the Son of God.

> *The church shines brightest when it aligns with the Son of God.*

Since we have no light within us, except what we receive from the Son of God, we are like the moon. We reflect the light from the Son. Since we merely reflect the light we receive into the darkness around us, we must be in position with the Son to reflect His full glory.

Recently, my wife and I were riding in the car when she looked into the night sky and said, "There is a full moon. That means everything is in alignment with the sun. At a full moon there are more babies conceived and birthed."

Our ministry is called *New Birth*, a name God gave us because our purpose is to be a birthing place for the kingdom of God. Fulfilling that assignment means we must live in alignment with the King. The life of God comes forth when we as His people walk in correct alignment with kingdom processes and deliverance. Our relationship causes us to come alive to God.

Did you know that the moon controls the ocean's tides? Consider for a moment that spiritual and prophetic implications exist. When the church, as symbolized by the moon, is out of alignment with the Son, as symbolized by the sun, the earth can be swept away in a tide of destruction due to sin.

## The Symbol of the Stars

Jesus Christ included stars when He spoke of signs of the end of the age in Luke 21:7, 25:

> So they asked Him, saying, "Teacher, but when will these things be? And what sign will there be when these things are about to take place?"...And there will be signs in the sun, in the moon, and in the stars....

Stars represent the ministries of the church—tied into the promise to Abraham found in Exodus 32:13:

> "Remember Abraham, Isaac, and Israel, Your servants, to whom You swore by Your own self, and said to them, 'I will multiply your descendants as the stars of heaven; and all this land that I have spoken of I give to your descendants, and they shall inherit it forever.'"

You can only see stars at night. Stars help the lost find their way in darkness. The political and economic order of our nation and the entire world are in darkness. Stars are not TV stars or TV preachers, but individuals who roll up their sleeves in the trenches and do the work of ministry. Ministers around the globe are having a great impact, regardless of whether they work in full-time ministry or at a nine-to-five job. These men and women bring illumination into dark places, proclaiming

31

through their hard work and godly attitudes: "I'm not here to get a paycheck, I'm here to alter the course of this nation and this world."

> *His tail drew a third of the stars of heaven and threw them to the earth. And the dragon stood before the woman who was ready to give birth, to devour her Child as soon as it was born. She bore a male Child who was to rule all nations with a rod of iron. And her Child was caught up to God and His throne.* (Revelation 12:4–5)

## LABOR PAINS

God is bringing forth a corporate child. Paul said, *"My little children, for whom I labor in birth again until Christ is formed in you"* (Galatians 4:19). Some believers don't get mad as easily as they once did. Others no longer find time to gossip. They say, "I'm on assignment for the kingdom of God, and I don't have time for gossip. I'm going to walk in the calling and purpose God has ordained for my life."

As a corporate body, we're saying, "We've got a world assignment and nations to subdue. We've got to bring things in order." Over the last few years we have been in labor. God is forming Christ within us, not to birth us as a bunch of individuals. He intends the body of Christ to be one.

On December 11, 2004, the more than twenty-five thousand believers united in heart and purpose who marched through the streets of Atlanta were individuals who came together as one great corporate body. The march shook principalities—which created an outpouring of persecution and lies against us.

There is an old expression: "If you hit a dog, it'll holler." What is out of order with God will make a lot of noise. Whatever is in darkness must be brought into the marvelous light of gospel truth. The world is suffering in darkness and pain. It's filled with devastation and sin. The Bible says the earth is in travail as it waits for the church to come into maturity.

> *For I consider that the sufferings of this present time are not worthy to be compared with the glory which shall be revealed in us. For the earnest expectation of the creation eagerly waits for the revealing of the sons of God.*
>
> (Romans 8:18–19)

The creation is groaning—even the bottom of the ocean is shaking, moving, shifting, expecting the sons and daughters of God to be revealed. Tornadoes, hurricanes, and disturbances in nature have been occurring on all corners of the globe.

> ### *The whole earth waits for the true sons of God to come forth.*

It's been so long since the earth heard the voice of God that it's causing a groaning as the earth aligns itself.

> *For the creation was subjected to futility, not willingly, but because of Him who subjected it in hope; because the creation itself also will be delivered from the bondage of corruption into the glorious liberty of the children of God.*
>
> (Romans 8:20–21)

The whole earth is waiting and travailing for the true sons of God to come forth. We're lining up—getting into place, moving into alignment, and getting ready to come forth. Just as Lazarus came forth from the grave, the church of the living God will rise up and take its place in the purposes of God. The earth knows all about it, and it is eager, longing for it to happen.

When the people of God come together, He stands among them, empowering them. Look at Psalm 82:

> *God [elohim] stands in the congregation of the mighty [el]; He judges among the gods. How long will you judge unjustly, and show partiality to the wicked? Selah. Defend the poor and fatherless; do justice to the afflicted and needy. Deliver the poor and needy; free them from the hand of the wicked. They do not know, nor do they understand; they walk about in darkness; all the foundations of the earth are unstable. I said, "You are gods, and all of you are children of the Most High. But you shall die like men, and fall like one of the princes." Arise, O God, judge the earth; for You shall inherit all nations.* (Psalm 82:1–8)

The original Hebrew text says, *Elohim* stands in the congregation of *el*. Whenever we come together and worship, God not only stands *with* us, but He also stands *in* us. We reflect His nature and presence. He is standing in the congregation of *gods* with a small "g." You are His representatives here on earth, and therefore He asks, "How long are you going to judge unrighteously?"

God is telling us, "I'm trying to get you to walk so holy that you won't have to pass out tracts or wear a T-shirt to make it known you are Christians. Your holy lives will speak so loudly that everyone will know. People will see God in you.

Verse 5 says, *"They do not know, nor do they understand; they walk about in darkness; all the foundations of the earth are unstable."* In ancient times ships didn't have today's modern instrumentation to navigate. They were completely dependent upon the stars to guide them through the darkness and on to safe harbors. If clouds covered the stars and the sailors couldn't see them, they would have to drop anchor and wait until the skies cleared. If not, they might be tossed about aimlessly.

The implication here is that you are a star, and your life is supposed to be light in the darkness of the world. If you do not live up to your promise, if your light becomes dim or goes out, then the peoples of the world will become unstable. They will be tossed about.

That's why the text says, *"And so all of the foundations of the earth are unstable."* We, as the church of Jesus Christ, are ordained to light the darkness, to illuminate the way through rough waters and dark nights. If we do not do so, we're responsible for the instability that follows.

> **As the church, we are to light the darkness and show the way.**

Too few of us realize we're the little *"el."* We become content to hear sermons preached Sunday after Sunday about how happy we should be just to be saved. "Aren't you glad you're not going to hell?" Yet, your family is not saved, and you feel no responsibility to shine the light of truth to them.

The seas and waves are crashing, uncertainty is everywhere, and men's hearts are failing them for fear, just as the

Bible predicted. (See Luke 21:26.) The Bible foretells the terror of our time; and after 9/11 all we hear about is *terror*. Terror alerts rule our lives; and just walking through the airport and boarding a plane feels like an assault against our self. We live in fear of people who are willing to blow themselves up just to kill us. Every time a football game or a political rally is held, everyone has to be checked for bombs, guns, and knives. Men's hearts are failing in fear, suspicious to the point that we're becoming one nation under *surveillance*.

In this stressful hour, it is important that we hold fast to our freedoms. The powers of the heavens will be shaken. They're being shaken right now, but the righteous will not be shaken, says the Word of God. *"Surely he will never be shaken; the righteous will be in everlasting remembrance"* (Psalm 112:6).

In this hour, God is speaking. Perhaps you once ran and played and lived a worldly life and felt that God was winking at you and overlooking your sin. You may have felt you were getting away with sin in the past, but you won't get away with sin today. God is speaking! In the book of Hebrews we are warned:

> *See that you do not refuse Him who speaks. For if they did not escape who refused Him who spoke on earth, much more shall we not escape if we turn away from Him who speaks from heaven, whose voice then shook the earth; but now He has promised, saying, "Yet once more I shake not only the earth, but also heaven."*　(Hebrews 12:25–26)

God is saying that once more the earth will be shaken, as it was in Noah's day. But much more will happen: the heavens will be shaken as well. Everything that can be shaken will be shaken. Why? To remove those things that can be shaken, so what cannot be shaken may remain.

> *Now this, "Yet once more," indicates the removal of those things that are being shaken, as of things that are made, that the things which cannot be shaken may remain. Therefore, since we are receiving a kingdom which cannot be shaken, let us have grace, by which we may serve God acceptably with reverence and godly fear.* (Hebrews 12:27–28)

Maybe you're thinking this sounds like bad news. It is, for the wicked. Hebrews 12:27 changes tone. We are members of a kingdom that will escape the shakings that are coming to the world. And when we are properly aligned with our head, Jesus Christ, we will be unshakable. We will see the Son of man coming in a cloud with power and great glory, coming for us, His bride.

## LIFT UP YOUR HEAD

Before His return, Christ's body will come together in unity of spirit and purpose. You might recall the passage in Ezekiel 37 where the dry bones arose and started coming together. That will be us, the living church of Jesus Christ. When those bones come together, it will be with a great noise. Today, a great noise is coming from around the world as the earth shakes. In time, the world will see His appearance.

When you see the earth begin to shake, rock, and reel—when mountains seem to fall into the sea, and people's hearts fail under the strain of worldwide terrorism—don't get depressed. Don't let CNN, ABC, and all the ungodly voices of the world confuse you. God says, "When these things begin to happen, look up and lift up your head." He is coming quickly!

So lift your head, look up and see Him:

*Lift up your heads, O you gates! And be lifted up, you everlasting doors! And the King of glory shall come in. Who is this King of glory? The LORD strong and mighty, the LORD mighty in battle. Lift up your heads, O you gates! Lift up, you everlasting doors! And the King of glory shall come in. Who is this King of glory? The LORD of hosts.*

(Psalm 24:7–10)

Jesus Christ is the King of glory, so lift up your head! The King of Glory is about to *bust up* in here. Why get excited? Because your redemption is near!

> ### Lift up your head because your redemption is near!

*Redeemed* means "to buy back." God is saying, "I'm about to get everything you lost and give it back to you." I'm here to tell you that your promise of prosperity and plenty is right here waiting for you right now. As your light shines brightly as a star, all nations shall be drawn to the light of your rising. (See Isaiah 60:3.)

The wait is over. There is no more time for division within our churches. Most nonbelievers don't even know what the church is supposed to look like when they join one. They just know where to go when they're in need. But we have power to help them, because we're aligning ourselves with the Son!

When you're disbursed throughout the community and the world, you're still connected in the spirit with the body of Christ. At work you are a star, shining brightly with your attitude, wisdom, love, and work ethic. You show the world how it should be living. And when they say, "What about all of those people dying in tsunamis, hurricanes, and other natural disasters?" you say, "Look up, for your redemption is near!"

There are some in your church family who have paid a dear price to walk with God. I'm here to tell you that everything He promised is about to come forth. Others have had to struggle to come out of sin and darkness. It's not been easy for them, but they've pushed through mountains and have made it.

God is speaking truth that will revolutionize the church of Jesus Christ. We are to ready to set a paradigm for the nations. We are ready to start pulling, shifting, and moving things into greater alignment with God's purpose and plan. When things happen, don't hang your head in shame. God says, "When you see these things beginning to happen, look up."

Just as the underground plates that form the foundation of the earth shifted, causing a great tsunami, we are about to experience a shift in the spiritual realm. God is about to show Himself through His people as never before. Get ready to shine with the light of God's truth and power in a way you never dreamed possible. He's also going to place abundance, blessing, and spiritual gifts back into your hands. The only requirement is that we walk together: one Lord, one faith, one baptism.

Something marvelous is happening in the spiritual realm right now, so lift up your head and let your light shine. God says, "This will be your finest hour."

# CHAPTER 3

# A MANDATE FOR THE NATION

Recently, we invited teenagers from area schools to attend a special youth service we called *The Boyfriend/Girlfriend Thing*. We got school principals involved by awarding a large cash prize to the school with the most students in attendance. But when a parade of more than eight thousand teenagers thundered through the doors of the church, packing out our sanctuary and overflow rooms, all we could do was bless God.

Some considered it a sign that God was pleased with our determination to take back what the devil had stolen. The Lord was anointing our efforts in order to affirm our determination and consecrate our vows. As a church, we refuse to limit our impact upon our high schools just because someone shouts "separation of church and state!" at us. We've been told the church has no place in the school system, but we refuse to accept that. We are taking back our children, because these young people are a gift of God to *us*—not to the devil, not to the world, and not to the state.

We're making an impact by imprinting the gospel upon the lives of children. You see, we fully intend to take back our young people—every last one of them. The devil and world cannot have them.

Our parents are rising up and taking back their rightful place in the community and in the lives of these kids. They refuse to be delayed and will not be deterred. They've begun volunteering at the schools, walking the halls, getting to know the teachers and the curriculum, and making their presence— and authority—known.

The principal of our local high school is a member of our church. Recently, our local high school was given the highest rating in the nation from the Air Force ROTC. People have a tendency to think that because our children have black, brown, or cocoa skin that they can't retain knowledge; but at Lithonia High School we believe that's a lie. Others have tried to say our kids don't know how to behave at school. We're raising the standard, because nobody can rise to low expectations.

> *Young people are a gift of God to us—not to the devil or the world.*

The children at our schools praise God every day and night; even with separation of church and state. Something wonderful is going on!

The devil has tried to convince us that we've lost our children. You should have been here the night they came thundering through those doors. Our children are not lost. Thousands of the redeemed children of the Lord marched in. Why? They were making a statement. They want to do the right thing, to live right. With our help, and with the help of the Lord, they're going to take it to the next level at Lithonia High School.

## Opposing the Myth of Separation of Church and State

As you have probably noticed, God has strongly communicated to me His displeasure with our nation's growing acceptance of the mythical "separation of church and state" heresy. I am convinced this so-called separation was never the intent of our nation's founding fathers—it is merely a device gradually created by an errant Supreme Court totally apart from historical precedent, tradition, or even the will of the people.

We understand our calling in God to be leaders to the nation in matters concerning God's kingdom, and that includes boldly confronting anything—*anything*—that raises its head against the authority of God and His Word. Paul was blunt and to the point when he wrote:

> *For the weapons of our warfare are not carnal but mighty in God for pulling down strongholds, casting down arguments and every high thing that exalts itself against the knowledge of God, bringing every thought into captivity to the obedience of Christ.* (2 Corinthians 10:4–5)

Our rejection of this false doctrine of separation is not new. In 1997, a young student was stabbed to death during a fight at Southwest DeKalb High School, a local magnet school for gifted students. We were asked by various leaders in the public school system and in the county judicial system

43

to conduct a rally for the heartbroken students. The meeting took place during school hours despite Supreme Court rulings prohibiting public schools from sponsoring religious services.

One of our members was DeKalb County's top law enforcement officer at that time. He stood up before the entire student body of sixteen hundred students, who had all voluntarily attended the service, and said, "Here we are in defiance of the Supreme Court, calling on the name of Jesus Christ."

## Hundreds Were Saved

I preached for twenty-five minutes. I began by telling the students, "God told me to come here because He has chosen Southwest DeKalb [High School] to be His kingdom of high schools." I told them that God had ordained them to be a special group of students and that we had gathered together to sanctify that ordination. Then I said, "I want you to understand that this is the reason we are here. This is the reason the school board allowed us to come. This is the reason that God has ordained this day."

> No "separation of church and state" exists. God made everything.

At the end of that seventy-five-minute "motivational assembly," students came forward by the hundreds to confess their faith in Jesus and to receive prayer. As you can imagine, the legal director for the Georgia office of the American Civil Liberties Union (ACLU) was not pleased. Nevertheless, we refused to back down from the truth of God's Word. We will not be deterred, for no "separation of church and state" exists, because God made everything.

## A MANDATE TO CHALLENGE
### AND TO CHANGE

We challenged the state for control of our children in the local high schools, and we've made a significant impact on the lives of our kids. As a body of believers, God has given us a mandate to challenge and change the status quo. The Lord has called us to take on not just the schools, but many of the most powerful institutions on the American political scene, and we have only begun to fight.

The passion I have received from the Lord (and the passion that I want to impress upon you) is the passion to step into public and religious arenas at God's direction. Put everything on the line by challenging ungodly systems that hold people in bondage. It is time to allow God to strip away timidity and openly take a stand.

God is searching for a people who will step out into the water, based only on His promise. That kind of Christian is in short supply today. We have allowed the government to slap us on the wrists and tell us, "You can't pray in school. You can't talk about God." Yet when we make the effort to talk to government officials and school administrators individually about the problems they face, we find that many of them know they need God in the schools, in the public arena, in government and in their own personal lives. They know sometimes better than we that the nation needs God.

They are looking for somebody to stand up and challenge the misguided "powers that be" who have attempted to set aside the decrees of God.

Not only has God led our church to take a stand to reclaim our schools and our children, we've also stood against the pressure of ungodly political alliances and publicly confronted their error in the face of great pressure to compromise.

### Twice We Confronted the Nation of Islam

We were also compelled by the Lord to lead a number of like-minded churches in taking a stand against two initiatives of the Nation of Islam. That stand put us on the front pages of many American newspapers. The first incident happened when Minister Louis Farrakhan issued a nationwide call to all African Americans to attend the so-called Million Man March in Washington. (Nowhere near that number showed up, but for some reason the number stuck.)

In response, we held a news conference and listed what became known nationally as the Nine Reasons that every Christian—regardless of color or race—should boycott the event sponsored by the Nation of Islam. Obviously, this didn't make us too popular with the Nation of Islam or even with those segments of the Christian African American population that put loyalty to race and ethnicity ahead of loyalty to the blood of Christ and the kingdom of God.

Once again we issued the Nine Reasons when Minister Farrakhan called on African Americans to observe a national Day of Atonement (this day is honored by some segments of Islam as well as by observing Jews) by boycotting work, school, and shopping activities. The event was openly billed as a celebration in honor of the second anniversary of the so-called Million Man March. I told the media:

> We cannot support anything that does not have Christ as the center. We have great respect for Minister Farrakhan, but within the confines of the Nation of Islam you will find that it was established as an anti-Christian movement.

Again, this didn't sit well with the sponsors of the event, including some prominent Christian clergymen (some of them from my own denominational family) who failed to recognize the Bible-based differences between the Nation of Islam and

### God's Word is true whether it is politically correct or not.

the kingdom of God. It doesn't matter—God's Word is true whether it is politically correct or not.

All we are doing is pursuing the vision God gave me as the leader of New Birth Missionary Baptist Church. This pursuit of our destiny can only happen as I impart my heart and vision to others. The mobilization and follow-up on these issues are carried out by my spiritual sons and daughters. Again, this is the key for every local body of Christ who wants to fulfill God's commission to take over instead of being overtaken. We must raise up sons and daughters of the kingdom instead of pouring ourselves into programs, activities, and religious movements outside of God's will.

### A RADICAL MESSAGE IS RISING

Any leader inspired by Satan to lead a rebellion against God must also strike out at the foundation of God's order on the earth. It is no accident that the church is being pressured to come into agreement with powerful gay lobby groups or face the consequences. Every segment of governmental power, from the Congress to the executive branch to the Supreme Court, is being lobbied, pressured, and wooed to support the anti-Christ, anti-Bible, gay rights cause. Hawaii has passed laws recognizing domestic partnerships for homosexuals, and corporations by the thousands are beginning to cave in to strong gay demands. It is all part of the satanic agenda to undermine the foundation of marriage and the home that God first instituted in the Book of Genesis.

I hear a radical message rising up out of the kingdom of God from a small minority. More and more voices are crying, "Enough is enough!" It is clear to anyone with eyes to see and ears to hear that we are about to cross an invisible boundary into a state of major change and uncertainty. Over the last few decades our societal and governmental structures have placed their trust not in God, but in institutions of men: such as the Federal Reserve and the United Nations.

Too many pastors preach about the rapture as if it were an easy way out of a difficult and increasingly dark world. Yet it is clear that this is not where God is moving right now. Yes, He is coming, but He is not coming to "rapture" or "snatch away" His scared and overwhelmed people and then leave the planet in cinders. He is coming to take over and rule and reign with a bride, the truly grown-up church, that has neither spot nor wrinkle. In fact, we have a wonderful opportunity to rise up in God's glory right now because He is pulling down everything that has exalted itself against His Word.

## HOUSECLEANING

When I was a child, my mother used to spend a great deal of time cleaning and preparing our home for special events. She would tackle the rooms, closets, kitchen, and us kids with fierce and unrelenting abandon. No one got in her way. Something similar is happening in the church of Jesus Christ as He makes preparation for His appearing.

> *God is pulling down everything exalted against His Word.*

God is cleaning house, but much of the church is not making herself ready. It is my burning passion to see His face, but I am afraid that a lot of church folk are going to be very much offended by the way God is going to act. It's going to get even tougher for many church leaders.

Judgment always begins in the house of God. (See 1 Peter 4:17.) Right now He is separating the sheep from the goats just as Jesus described the separation of the nations in Matthew 25:32. He is about to raise up new leaders who have ears to hear the new sound of His Spirit.

The leaders we had in the sixties, seventies, eighties, and even in the nineties will not be the same leaders who take us into the troubled times we're about to face. The Father is seeking those who have been totally broken and are dead to self and selfish ambition. He is looking for "Joshua faith," not "Moses faith," in this new breed of leader.

Moses was one of the greatest leaders in the Bible, but even Moses had to wait until the water was parted to cross the Red Sea. Joshua was required by the Lord to step out into the flood waters of uncertainty while trusting God to stop the river Jordan. (See Joshua 3:11–17.)

## A Battle Cry

The American church is best known for her ambitious leaders who want to make a name for themselves. Many of us devote all of our energies to building our own kingdoms and religious monuments, often at the expense of others in the body of Christ. In true American fashion, many of our church leaders and televangelists often excel at self-promotion, hype, and pomp and circumstance, but fail miserably in the weightier matters of obedience to God, sacrifice, humility, service to others, and submission to God-ordained authority. That is about to change.

> *And they said, "Come, let us build ourselves a city, and a tower whose top is in the heavens; let us make a name for ourselves, lest we be scattered abroad over the face of the whole earth." But the LORD came down to see the city and the tower which the sons of men had built.*
>
> (Genesis 11:4–5)

It is time for a showdown; and it is God's turn to make His statement. Let me paint a picture for you by reminding you of the time God sent fire from heaven to consume Elijah's sacrifice and altar on Mount Carmel in front of four hundred priests of Baal while all of Israel watched. We need to take off our religious spectacles and stop thinking of this historical event in 1 Kings 18 as just a Bible story. It is a chilling prophetic picture of where the church and the nation are this very moment.

Israel was the "established church" of Elijah's day. It was a nation of people who had been set apart unto God many generations earlier. They still had all the traditions of their fathers in their memory, along with all the stories of God's provision recorded in the Law. But the people of God were chasing after other gods and other pursuits. Yet the day came when they were all summoned together to make a choice, and God made a clear division between what was His and what wasn't. (It is interesting to note that God isn't against highly visible and dynamic leaders—He just insists that they be elevated by His hand, not by the hand of man, and that those leaders dynamically direct His people toward His purposes and not their own.)

The fire is coming again, first to God's set-apart people, because judgment begins with the house of God. (See 1 Peter 4:17.) Then it will come to the nation. Our society has defiantly turned away from its godly roots and has busied itself building monuments and laws to honor man's ingenuity over God's. While the sin mounts higher and higher, we as a nation sink deeper and deeper into a moral and financial bankruptcy of our own making. Meanwhile, God is about to divide the church and the nation, to make a clear separation between what is His and what isn't. Most Christians have no idea what is coming.

There is a war going on, and we need to take the focus off ourselves and put it back on God where it belongs. You and I need to realize He has placed us on the front lines of this battle whether we like it or not.

Part of our problem is that we tend to stay in only one lane of God's Word—the "bless me" lane. We forget what Paul said about the complete purpose of God's Word: *"All Scripture is given by inspiration of God, and is profitable for **doctrine**, for **reproof**, for **correction**, for **instruction** in righteousness"* (2 Timothy 3:16, emphasis added). Now I don't remember seeing the crowds line up at the door an hour ahead of time to hear a preacher talk about reproof or correction. I think I know why.

### Called to His Purpose

Most of us keep our focus fixed on our personal situations in church meetings and Bible studies. But if we don't understand the greater corporate purposes of God, then our confusion can become painful. Why? Because we won't be able to see how our lives fit into the larger picture of what God is orchestrating. The Bible gives us a hint about how we fit into God's larger scope of attention:

> *And we know that all things work together for good to those who love God, to those who are the called according to His purpose.* (Romans 8:28)

Too often we become obsessed with building our own kingdoms and making a name for ourselves, when God calls us to lift up His name and build up His kingdom. Our wrong motives and selfish personal agendas sabotage our best efforts.

> *Then His disciples came and said to Him, "Do You know that the Pharisees were offended when they heard this saying?" But He answered and said, "Every plant which My heavenly Father has not planted will be uprooted. Let them alone. They are blind leaders of the blind. And if the blind leads the blind, both will fall into a ditch."*
>
> (Matthew 15:12–14)

The eleventh chapter of the book of Genesis describes a people who wanted to make a name for themselves. They decided to do so by building a tower up into the heavens (we call it the Tower of Babel). They all spoke one language in the days immediately following the great flood, and they came into agreement to build a tower. What those people were really trying to

*God calls us to lift up His name and build up His kingdom.*

do was show God that they didn't need or want Him. They could reach the heavens on their own, without His help or permission.

The Hebrew word *migdal* is translated "tower" in this passage, but its fuller meaning reveals the real motives of the people. According to *Strong's Exhaustive Concordance*, *migdal* can mean a rostrum, a castle, or a pulpit; it comes from a root word that means "to make large (as in body, mind, estate or honor, also in pride), to advance, boast, bring up, exceed, excellent, and to increase, lift up, magnify, pass, promote." It is derived from definitions and root meanings for tower.

## The "Attitude" Prince

The vision for this tower required a leader; and Nimrod arrived on the scene.

> *Cush begot Nimrod; he began to be a mighty one on the earth. He was a mighty hunter before the LORD.*
>
> (Genesis 10:8–9)

Nimrod, the son of Cush, not only led the people in the building project, but he also led them in developing a bad attitude: "We will not allow anything like a flood to come and devastate us again. Now if we agree to build a tower and rally around it as we ascend into the heavens..." Not only did they take on the mentality that Adam and Eve had (desiring to know good and evil), they also were moving in the same exact sin (wanting to be like God, but without His help or permission). They were not just trying to be like God—they wanted to be God!

We are trying to build a Tower of Babel in our day, too. We are trying to be like God—or to be better than He is. If you haven't noticed, America is coming into agreement with all types of ungodly notions. We are trying to use the science and technology God gave us to do things that only God can do, including the act of creating life (though we've only been able to clone something from what already exists). We want to extend life through medicine to make up for our unwillingness to live and eat with wisdom. We don't want to live disciplined lives that include regular exercise and healthy diets, and we refuse to take care of the temple of the Holy Spirit. We want to cling to our smoking habits; we gamble that if we get lung cancer, we can get a transplant.

We are trying desperately to extend our lifespans today, and you might ask, "What is wrong with that?" On the surface there is nothing wrong with it. But the real theology and personal motivation behind this push in medicine is that we are trying to eliminate God and His laws. He gave us the original "long-life plan" centuries ago, and it consists of a godly life, wise eating habits, moderation in all things, respect for parents and those in authority, and the determination to love the Lord our God with all of our being.

We abuse the creative powers God gave us. Instead of following God's way, we cheat. We have pills that blast fat, so we don't have to exercise. We've invented sugar and fat substitutes so we can eat unhealthy foods without gaining weight. We don't rest on the Sabbath, we don't love our neighbor as ourselves, and we certainly don't take care of the temple of the Holy Spirit. We are trying to usurp the system and processes of God.

## A Rebellious Nation

An honest survey of our society reveals that we are trying to become God. We're trying to live up to our own propaganda about man being the "sum of all things." The idea is nothing new—the Greeks had the same philosophy. We are trying to rule our own destiny; even born-again Christians have adopted the secular viewpoint that the church is supposed to join hands with any outside group claiming to have even the slightest of good intentions. Tremendous pressure has been exerted on us to link up with everyone from the NAACP to the Hundred Black Men and the Hundred White Men; from fund-raisers for Greek collegiate sororities and fraternities to virtually every civic organization in our communities, including the Kiwanis Club, the Key Club, the Rotary Club, and so on.

Without question, many of these organizations are doing commendable work of great value in our communities. I'm thankful they exist, but honestly, the only reason they exist is because the church has failed to fulfill her destiny in the earth. Many times we think we must join together and work hand in hand to make our communities a better place; but I have to tell you that according to God's Word, that popular belief is not true! Let me explain why not:

When we say that the church must work hand in hand with these organizations for good, we automatically make God and His eternal kingdom equal to all of these man-made, secular organizations. We must understand that according to the Scriptures, we are the head as redeemed ambassadors of Christ. As the corporate body of Christ in the earth, we are literally the only "living thing" on this earth meant and equipped to straighten out every problem and every concern of mankind. But we must do it God's way.

God's way is centered on absolute obedience and trust in Christ, the cross, and the life-changing power of the Holy Spirit. How many wonderful civic organizations can you name that would welcome those world-changing forces and beliefs into their meetings and activities? When we understand that, it becomes obvious that we can't work within the systems of the world. God has ordained a divine order for life, governments, and the church—and this order is invisible to the natural eye. Only those who are saved and baptized into this invisible kingdom can see the order and the arrangement of God.

The church has become so mixed up and pulled in different directions by the whims of men that we have gradually adopted secular views of God and depreciated Him to "next to nothing." In other words, He and His body are now viewed by Christians and non-Christians alike as just another organization.

> *God has ordained a divine order for life, government, and church.*

That should explain why it is very difficult for us to make a sacrifice of time, money, or personal commitment to God—we are already giving most of our time and resources to other "worthy organizations" outside the church. We justify it by saying, "Oh, they are making society better." In actuality, society has become worse because we have usurped the process of God. The most any man-centered organization can do, apart from Christ, is to apply a pretty bandage to a terminal carcinoma.

I appreciate many of these civic service organizations and the individuals who volunteer their time and resources to help others. They represent the best man has to offer outside of God and His order. But I am compelled by the Word of God to say that these individuals need to come into the house of God and lay down all their titles and agendas to take on the name "child of God." If we then joined together under the banner of Christ, all the nations of this earth would be blessed because we would tackle our tasks of service in both the power of God and the submitted and unified strength of man, the power of agreement demonstrated at the Tower of Babel. That is God's intent. That is the process of God.

> **If we join together under the banner of Christ, all nations will be blessed.**

If you become angry and agitated by that process, then so be it. Perhaps that shows how far out in the world you are. The only way to change the ills and hurts of the world genuinely and permanently is to change the hearts of people and transform their thinking through the renewing power of God's Word.

## THE GLOBAL VILLAGE

The community of man—the "global village of the flesh"—is coming into agreement. We are essentially rallying around our common desire to build a tower of power outside of God's kingdom and God's process. If we put representatives of every known civic, political, and activist group in one building, they would all fight and argue with one another until a Christian dared to stand up and say: "Christ is the answer!" In a split second we would see every one of those people who were at one another's throats an instant before suddenly unite with one voice to shout down and belittle their "common enemy." The church finds unity in her faith in Jesus Christ. The world finds unity in its hatred and fear of Jesus Christ.

If we examine the way we have built up and elevated the power of our centers of culture and government, we will see that our society has established a clear pattern of usurping the authority of God in every sphere of life. The book of Genesis tells the story of the Tower of Babel and shows what happens when men try to be god themselves. It also explains why we have so many different nations and languages today.

> And the Lord said, "Indeed the people are one and they all have one language, and this is what they begin to do; now nothing that they propose to do will be withheld from them. Come, let Us go down and there confuse their language, that they may not understand one another's speech." So the Lord scattered them abroad from there over the face of all the earth, and they ceased building the city. Therefore its name is called Babel, because there the Lord confused the language of all the earth; and from there the Lord scattered them abroad over the face of all the earth.
>
> (Genesis 11:6–9)

Why did God come down to Babel to confuse the language of the descendants of Noah and scatter them across the earth? Because of human disobedience. God had already judged the human race with the flood of judgment in Noah's day, yet He had to split the still-rebellious human race into many nations and language groups several generations later. He would soon abandon His dealings with the many nations and instead single out a descendant of Noah's son Shem to raise up one nation to save the rest:

> *Now the Lord had said to Abram: "Get out of your country, from your family and from your father's house, to a land that I will show you. I will make you a great nation; I will bless you and make your name great; and you shall be a blessing. I will bless those who bless you, and I will curse him who curses you; and in you all the families of the earth shall be blessed."* (Genesis 12:1–3)

We have forgotten that God said, *"I will..."* Look closely at this passage again and remember that this is an eternal promise. God did not say Abram was to join with all the civic organizations of the world to make all the nations blessed. God said in essence, "I am going to do a whole lot of things through you, My people, the nation of Israel, whom I have chosen. In you all the other nations that I have scattered shall be blessed. That is My plan. This is My process. Now you don't have to do anything other than be obedient to Me, because I am going to do everything else." Somehow the church has forgotten that God said, "I will."

> *God has said, "I will do it." We only have to be obedient to Him.*

God has already done everything that needs to be done on this earth and in this country. All He has called us to do is be obedient. We think God needs help because we are not being obedient, and as a consequence, we are not seeing His provision. We run out to join up with everybody else outside

God's house to fix things when God never told us, "Join up with everybody else."

I am not saying these organizations and the people in them are evil or bad. The problem is that when we join up with everybody outside God's order and absolute rule, we start to compromise. In fact, not only do we compromise, but we also dilute what God has said. It is unavoidable. The only way a kingdom based upon absolute truth and the absolute rule of God can come into agreement with anything less is to water things down.

Follow me as we review the progression of man's error and God's sovereignty...

## Spirit of Compromise

Everybody has an opinion today. Listen to the evening news on television and radio. Watch the talk shows during the day (if you dare). The reason we have so many outrageous talk shows today is because everybody has an opinion, but nobody has a standard. The clear contrast between the order of God and the order of the world is revealed in Genesis 10 (Noah) and 11 (the Tower of Babel). This contrast is becoming clear in our day, too.

We are living in a deadly season of deception, and the church has created an environment of gullibility to deception by failing to teach the Word of God without compromise. Christians are quicker to rally around the problems of society than the answer of Christ. We gravitate toward those who claim to have answers today because we can touch them, we can see their faces, and we can admire their human abilities.

All the while God remains invisible and distant to us because we do not know Him.

Various members and factions within the church have argued with one another, and many Christian leaders have had problems with me because I oppose joining arms with outside organizations for popular pro-black causes such as the so-called Million Man March and the Day of Atonement activities sponsored by Rev. Louis Farrakhan and the Nation of Islam. My critics cry, "We are tired of the killing. We are tired of the drugs and the corruption." I am tired of all of that too; but I'm not tired of Jesus. He has never failed us; we have failed Him. He is the answer to all of our problems, but the solutions will only come when we do things His way.

Leaders like Louis Farrakhan can rise up with a message of hope mixed with liberal doses of racial hatred, division, and devotion to Islam, and they still win substantial support from Christians. Why? Because Christians have failed to obey God's call to follow Christ's example of self-sacrifice. Many of us don't want to take the painful steps necessary to leave our comfortable suburban houses to do what God has ordained in order to supernaturally meet needs in the mean streets of the inner city. We prefer our quiet neighborhoods and our exciting church meetings ten miles away from our true place of divine service. We have trouble stepping across the property line to share the message of Jesus with the neighbor we see every day!

## DEADLY DECEPTION

We have compromised on our jobs and with our personal priorities. We carefully avoid any mention of the Christ who redeemed and transformed us because we are afraid we will get fired. Why? Because we think a man in the flesh hired us, totally forgetting that God's Word says it is God who gives us the power to get wealth. (See Deuteronomy 8:18.) God gives us our jobs and vocations so that we can be witnesses, not so that He

> *God gives us our jobs and vocations so that we can be witnesses.*

can meet our needs. He has already taken care of our needs according to Matthew 6:

> *No one can serve two masters; for either he will hate the one and love the other, or else he will be loyal to the one and despise the other. You cannot serve God and mammon. Therefore I say to you, do not worry about your life, what you will eat or what you will drink; nor about your body, what you will put on. Is not life more than food and the body more than clothing? Look at the birds of the air, for they neither sow nor reap nor gather into barns; yet your heavenly Father feeds them. Are you not of more value than they? Which of you by worrying can add one cubit to his stature? So why do you worry about clothing? Consider the lilies of the field, how they grow: they neither toil nor spin; and yet I say to you that even Solomon in all his glory was not arrayed like one of these. Now if God so clothes the grass of the field, which today is, and tomorrow is thrown into the oven, will He not much more clothe you, O you of little faith? Therefore do not worry, saying, "What shall we eat?" or "What shall we drink?" or "What shall we wear?" For after all these things the Gentiles seek. For your*

*heavenly Father knows that you need all these things. But seek first the kingdom of God and His righteousness, and all these things shall be added to you.* (Matthew 6:24–33)

We live our lives in just as much pain and anguish as the non-Christians around us because we have forgotten our Source. We are ripe for deception by anybody who dares to stand up in front of the media claiming some kind of authority or power to make our lives easier. The problem is that we know more about our problems than we do about God's Word. As a result, we fall for the temptation to follow Satan's latest pied piper into oblivion.

I want us to understand what God is saying today. Nimrod foreshadows the last great world ruler who will rise up just before God descends to the earth to usher in a millennial reign. Nimrod appeared on the scene just before God called Abram out from among the Gentiles to bring him into the Promised Land. A flood of judgment had already destroyed the world once, but Noah was saved and his descendants multiplied. Then mankind revolted against God under the leadership of someone empowered by Satan just before God was to perform the promise. Nimrod the false messiah inspired such an ungodly move of unity that God Himself came down to deal with it.

We are at that point again.

Something or somebody is about to be elevated in the earth, and we are not going to be able to handle it by ourselves. Therefore God will once again come down to handle it Himself just before He fulfills His promise. And when He comes, He will come with fire.

## A Coming World Leader

In the midst of a godly movement to call men back to their God-ordained roles as true men, protectors, and leaders in the home, there are two counterfeit movements in the world. One, sponsored primarily by the lesbian and women's rights movements, seeks to make men like women. This group actively encourages men to step out of their leadership roles; it also strongly supports the abortion rights issue.

The second movement that largely dominates our culture and the media tells men they should cruelly dominate everything in their path with no fear, responsibilities, or consequences. This kind of hormone-driven macho manhood is what created the wrongs and the leadership void that produced the feminist movement in the first place! Neither extreme came from God.

My point is this: When mankind reaches the point where it says, *"Come, let us build ourselves a city, and a tower whose top is in the heavens; let us make a name for ourselves,"* as the people did in Genesis 11:4, then we can count on God coming to the city. Genesis 10:9 refers to Babel's ruler, Nimrod, as "the mighty hunter." God made him mighty on the earth, but Nimrod was guilty of the most blatant defiance of God. He absolutely refused to obey God's commands passed down through Noah from Adam. Nimrod's agenda defied God's command to subdue the earth under God's authority. He wanted to do it his way, apart from God's rule. He wanted to make a name for himself.

My friend, God has already given us a name, and it is the name of Jesus. We can pray in His name and command legions of demons to flee. All we have to do is humble ourselves under His mighty hand, and He will exalt us in due season. Our world, our nation, our cities, and our churches are out of order; and Daddy is about to step into the picture.

## GOD IS NOT COMING TO TAKE SIDES

We don't like to think about this kind of thing. We prefer to focus on our personal problems or how to get the blessings of God. "I just need a better job, or that house or car I've always wanted. Lord, all I need is four or five credit cards and a nice wardrobe so no one will know I'm living beyond my means 'by faith.'" We don't understand what is going on. We don't even have a clue that God's purposes for the earth are completed in Jesus Christ. And He will yet reign over all the earth as King of Kings and Lords of Lords! Whether it is politically correct or not, it is truth. God is coming to take over, not to take sides.

> *Jesus will reign over the earth as King of Kings and Lord of Lords.*

Satan's sin has eternally limited him to the role of the great imitator, the consummate counterfeit. He knows that one God-Man is to reign over the earth, so he is working tirelessly to impose upon our gullible world his own "god-man" as the destined world leader. The apostle Paul warned us that:

> *The coming of the lawless one is according to the working of Satan, with all power, signs, and lying wonders, and with all unrighteous deception among those who perish, because*

*they did not receive the love of the truth, that they might be
saved. And for this reason God will send them strong delu-
sion, that they should believe the lie, that they all may be
condemned who did not believe the truth but had pleasure in
unrighteousness.*          (2 Thessalonians 2:9–12)

Satan's counterfeit will assume the right to enforce all
of his dictates upon the people. Satan is setting the stage to
elevate his chosen leader in the public eye with lying signs
and wonders. That is why I am tired of emotional saints who
follow after emotional experiences. We must follow after
Christ, whether or not that includes an emotional experience
on any given day.

Our nation is overwhelmed with self-made turmoil and
trouble, and the people are looking for somebody to fill the
void—as long as it is not Jesus Christ. A vacuum is being created, ready for a great leader to fill. We are really looking for
a king. Americans want somebody—anybody—who can get
behind a microphone and say, "I'm going to fix it." We are
looking for a man because we don't understand the principles
and warnings of Genesis 12. We don't understand the promise, and even worse, we don't understand or acknowledge the
Promiser.

God is about to come down and visit this generation. He
is ready to strike down our resurrected Tower of Babel once
again, but this time He expects to find a remnant church, an
occupation force that is obedient, faithful, and full of glory and
power in the midst of the world's darkness. I am convinced
that a "new and improved" version of Nimrod is about to
rise up and draw an awed world together under his dazzling

show of charisma and power. Even the elect may be deceived if we are not firmly grounded in God's Word and if we aren't walking in intimate fellowship with the living God. (See Mark 13:22–23.)

### THE ANTICHRIST

Nimrod was a type and shadow of the Antichrist. He manifested or revealed his rebellion in the form of a confederacy and an open revolt against God. Genesis 10:9 says Nimrod *"was a mighty hunter before the LORD; therefore it is said, 'Like Nimrod the mighty hunter before the LORD.'"* The next verse says Nimrod's kingdom began with Babel. In other words, Nimrod pushed his own order and might right in the face of God—and the people of God went with him.

If we worship God in church on Sundays, yet go along with the world's godless agenda for righting society's wrongs Monday through Saturday, then we are in the order of Nimrod and in direct rebellion against the order of God!

The path I've just described leads to some complications that Daniel accurately predicted when he related the description of this false leader many centuries ago. This isn't my opinion; it is God's Word:

> *Then the king shall do according to his own will: he shall exalt and magnify himself above every god, shall speak blasphemies against the God of gods, and shall prosper till the wrath has been accomplished; for what has been determined shall be done. He shall regard neither the God of his fathers nor the desire of women, nor regard any god; for he shall exalt himself above them all.* (Daniel 11:36–37)

### DANGEROUS UNIONS

God chose God-fearing men and women to establish this nation. By His sovereignty God established the United States of America; yet because of the failures of the government and the people over the last few decades, we have dared to push God away instead of pulling God close. We have rejected truth and refused to inherit the hearts of our forefathers. Therefore, we have redrafted this nation into something other than

> *The solution to our pain is that we must get right with God.*

what God ordained it to be. The United States today is a mockery before God and a shadow of what we are ordained to be because we have become a nation in rebellion.

The solution to our pain is the same as it has always been: We must get right with God. What was true in Saul's day is still true today. Samuel warned King Saul:

> *Has the LORD as great delight in burnt offerings and sacrifices, as in obeying the voice of the LORD? Behold, to obey is better than sacrifice, and to heed than the fat of rams. For rebellion is as the sin of witchcraft, and stubbornness is as iniquity and idolatry. Because you have rejected the word of the LORD, He also has rejected you from being king.*
> (1 Samuel 15:22–23)

### BEWARE A GOVERNMENT GONE WRONG

In Saul's day, a government gone wrong nearly destroyed its people. The same thing is happening today. When the house of God—the church—sets itself in order according to God's Word, it will operate in supernatural power, vision, and authority as never before. The true church, the separated church, has every solution the world needs. We have the authority and supernatural wisdom needed to right society's wrongs and bring order wherever there is chaos; but it all begins at the cross.

We are not called to link arms with everybody and every organization that comes along with a good cause. Let them link arms with us after they lay aside their private agendas and alliances with devils, for we have something far superior to any good cause or noble end.

We are the people of God. We carry the Spirit of the Savior and the power of the Creator. We serve the Lamb of God who takes away the sins of the world. We come not merely in the name of a good cause or some nice idea. We come in the name of the King of Kings and the Lord of Lords!

CHAPTER 4

# A COMMUNITY MANDATE

O n Sunday, March 21, 1965, over three thousand marchers set out for Montgomery, walking twelve miles a day and sleeping in fields. By the time they reached the capitol building on Thursday, March 25, they were twenty-five thousand strong. A previous, smaller, more symbolic march was met by police with clubs, beatings, and blood. Still the marchers were undeterred. In less than five months following the march to Montgomery, President Lyndon Johnson signed the Voting Rights Act of 1965—pivotal legislation that began to level the mountain of racial injustice in America.

Back in the 1960s, Martin Luther King Jr. was called by God as a prophetic voice to lead a generation to liberty and change. The man with the name "King" was, in truth, a kingdom voice. In his generation, he was a sign and wonder given by God to lead a nation away from the darkness of hatred and the slavery of injustice, into the light of liberty and truth. His was a voice, not just for black folk, but for all people—and not just for Americans, but for people around the world.

King's voice had power, and his gift carried dominion. Yet, when he died, his voice passed away with him. Although the masses followed him in courageous action, they never caught his vision. His heart and spirit died with him. What God intended to be passed on to the generations that followed did not get passed on. We saw him as our leader, but he did not become our father. We heard the dream, we were stirred by its passion, but his spirit did not become our own. In this we have suffered great loss.

## Few Fathers

God does not see as we see, for His ways are not our ways. We tend to see only the time span in which we live, but He is a God of generations.

> *For He established a testimony in Jacob, and appointed a law in Israel, which He commanded our fathers, that they should make them known to their children; that the generation to come might know them, the children who would be born, that they may arise and declare them to their children.* (Psalm 78:5–6)

God spoke these words to four generations: the fathers were generation one. Their children were generation two. The children yet born were generation three. And their children were generation four. This suggests that when I address you, I am speaking to four generations. And when you listen to me, you listen as a representative of four generations.

Few in today's church understand the vital principle of *generational transfer.* Our ignorance causes us to remain one generation away from being extinct because we're not passing on what we have received from God. The dominion of the kingdom of God is not being given from one generation to the next. We're not passing the torch of truth, light, liberty, and power. We hear the "voice" of the fathers who have gone before us. But the dominion of kingdom authority is not being transferred because we have not caught the "spirit" of that voice.

> ## We must pass the torch of truth to the next generation.

Because we've been incapable of receiving generational transfers, we have few fathers. Paul said to the Corinthians, *"For though you might have ten thousand instructors in Christ, yet you do not have many fathers"* (1 Corinthians 4:15).

There are but a few voices that God has raised up to lead you in destiny. There are a whole lot of people who can teach you some things. But God has appointed only a few to convey a double portion of the Spirit of God upon your life through the power of faith.

Look at Malachi:

> *Remember the Law of Moses, My servant, which I com-*
> *manded him in Horeb for all Israel, with the statutes and*
> *judgments. Behold, I will send you Elijah the prophet before*
> *the coming of the great and dreadful day of the LORD. And*
> *he will turn the hearts of the fathers to the children, and the*
> *hearts of the children to their fathers, lest I come and strike*
> *the earth with a curse.* (Malachi 4:4–6)

After God spoke this, He stopped talking for four hundred years. It is the very last verse in the Old Testament. God was saying, "It's going to take you four hundred years to meditate on what I just said." The next words God speaks come from an angel. In Luke 1:17, we are informed that John the Baptist would come in the *"spirit and power of Elijah."*

God didn't say John would come in the spirit of Moses, Jeremiah, or Samuel. He said the spirit of Elijah. Doubtless you're familiar with the story of Elijah in 2 Kings 2 where Elijah asks Elisha, his young prophetic apprentice, what he wants. Elisha boldly responds that he wants a double portion of the elder prophet's spirit. Elijah had the ability to transfer his powerful anointing on to another generation. Teachers can't do that. Only the fathers of movements of God can do that.

To receive this kind of transfer will require that you learn to wait patiently. It will not come quickly. Elisha had to wait until Elijah was taken up to heaven. He couldn't receive it while his spiritual father was alive.

> *As a father, I give my heart to my sons. We must unite in vision.*

Malachi 4:6 says God will turn the hearts of the fathers to the children, and the hearts of the children to the fathers. Generational transference is a matter of the heart. In other words, as a son I must catch or inherit the heart of my father. As a father, I must give my heart to my sons. Together we must be united in vision and voice.

## A GOD OF GENERATIONS

Ever since Adam, God has been after the heart of mankind. He is not seeking a perfect attendance record at church or a sinless life. Only one Man, Jesus Christ, could ever pull that off. But if you inherit the Father's heart, then He will move it from generation to generation in ever-expanding power and glory. It all depends on a transfer of the heart and Spirit of God. Success in the local church depends on a transfer of the heart of human leaders to those whom God places under their care.

Every generation is supposed to be better off than the last generation; but for the first time in history we are looking at a generation that is worse off than the generation that came before. It is all because they did not understand the inheritance of the heart and the transgenerational transfer of vision and knowledge. God wants to move from generation to generation.

The double portion Elisha received enabled him to do twice what Elijah had accomplished. This suggests that our children are destined to do more and go farther than we, their elders, ever could. If we are upsetting governments and shaking nations, imagine what the impact of our children will be if they catch our spirit.

God is not interested in just getting you saved, baptized, filled with the Holy Spirit, and moving in power. Yes, you need all of that. However, if you have all of those things but do not inherit the Father's heart (or your spiritual father's heart) and pass it on, you will not succeed in God's purpose for your life.

God isn't nearsighted as we are. His vision passes beyond the barrier of time to span generation after generation. He sees the beginning from the end. Even before the worlds were made, He could see His Son on the cross. He also saw you entering the world on the day you were born and reading these very words at this moment in time.

It should be no surprise to us that God moves among and upon men generationally as well. He is as interested in the well-being of your unborn great-granddaughter as He is in your welfare. The thing He has placed on your heart today will directly affect those who come after you in a later day.

We need to understand that God gives us children as a loan. The Bible tells us that children are God's inheritance, and He has given us the responsibility to raise them up to be like arrows shot into the future! (See Psalm 127.) Our sons and daughters must inherit our hearts. They must receive something of the mission and anointing God placed in our hearts.

> *God gives us children as a loan that we are responsible for.*

Otherwise these deposits from God will die, and our children will be doomed to start all over without an inheritance. (See Proverbs 13:22.)

Today, God is again pouring out the "spirit of Elijah," but this time He is pouring it over the body of Christ. He is looking for people who are unafraid to speak with a profound boldness and who will rightly divide the Word of truth.

The very last prophetic words God uttered in the Old Testament through Malachi were, *"Lest I come and strike the earth with a curse"* (Malachi 4:6). The curse was promised if the hearts didn't turn.

This world is already under a curse. It is evident in our downward spiraling statistics concerning divorce, abortion, incest, rape, violence, corruption, and scandal (even in the church). The greatest indictment of all is that in most cases, you can't tell the Christians apart from the non-Christians—we're all alike! A sad indictment of this generation.

## DEATH OF THE BLACK AMERICAN CHURCH

The American church essentially died around 1950—especially in the black community. That was when we decided to stop advancing, and instead live on yesterday's seeds and deeds. We started doing the same old thing while avoiding anything new in God. So here we are, still conducting 1950s-vintage spiritual warfare, while the devil has advanced to a new millennium. He is waging state-of-the-art warfare against a church that hasn't left the 1950s!

*God wants to impart greater authority to our sons and daughters.*

It is all because there is no order in the house. We are not shooting our children like arrows of God into the future. We haven't equipped them with our anointing, our knowledge, or their full godly inheritance.

God wants to impart greater authority than our own into His sons and daughters, but our religiosity and vain imaginations are blocking the way. For generations we have abandoned His pattern of the inheritance of the heart in our natural families and in the church, and the backwash of our neglect has poisoned the organizations, institutions, and morals of our society and nation even more.

I've gone into great detail about the importance of raising up sons and daughters in the kingdom and how this principle has become the foundation of my life and ministry. God intends to carry this pattern to the highest levels of the church and to every area of our society. In my own experience, I've noticed that God has taken my ministry to "sons" to a new level. Recently I was asked to speak at a conference where I found myself thinking, *Lord, did I miss You in this? Should I be at home?* I didn't even know what the Lord wanted me to say. In fact, I switched messages just before I stood to minister.

Evidently I landed on the message God wanted me to preach because that church has been in revival ever since that service. They told me later that the word that really spoke to them came through me. God set people free of lust and drugs, and He put marriages back together that night. Everybody was at the altar, on their faces before God.

## "That's My Daddy"

I realized God was up to something in my "fathering" ministry from the moment I arrived at that church. I had never met the pastor before, but when I walked into the church, shook this man's hand, and gave him a hug, we were immediately joined together in the Spirit. After I ministered in that powerful service, I was ready to go to the hotel and go to bed. I put on a jogging suit and sneakers for the ride back to the hotel, but God led me right back to the front of that church.

Even though it was midnight, the pastor had asked the congregation to wait for me.

This pastor stood up in front of his congregation and said, "The Lord spoke to me tonight, and I have heard something. I have never met this man before," he said as he turned toward me, "but that's my daddy." In that moment this church of more than five thousand began to leap for joy because they too heard the sound that was coming from my voice. That night the entire congregation and its pastor submitted to my spiritual headship—but not because I asked them to do so. Why did they do it? It was because they heard a word from the Holy Spirit.

There was no interview. There was no questioning. There was no debate or discussion. This pastor did not have to do it, but he heard a sound. I'm seeing this same process take place everywhere God sends me. Very often, just as soon as I finish ministering God's Word, a pastor will say, "Will you be my spiritual father? I realize I have to submit somewhere because I have to be covered. I hear that same thing you are hearing, but I need to be led." I can guarantee that I don't engineer these events. I don't know if you realize it, but this kind of thing can only happen when God is behind it.

## Laying the Foundation

My son Kody is supposed to do even greater things than I have done. I am supposed to build a platform upon which he will rise up and do even greater exploits. But if I poison him with a negative, ungodly heritage and hinder him by not providing him the spiritual nourishment he needs, he will not be able to do them. Instead, he will spend most of his life finding out who he is and undoing the evil I did to him in his early years. Now do you see why God's order is so important in the house?

It all begins with man. In the book of Genesis God established the man as the foundation for both the family and the church:

> *This is the history of the heavens and the earth when they were created, in the day that the LORD God made the earth and the heavens, before any plant of the field was in the earth and before any herb of the field had grown. For the LORD God had not caused it to rain on the earth, and there was no man to till the ground.* (Genesis 2:4–5)

God needed a man. There was mist to maintain the proper moisture, but there was no rain and no man to move forward. God needed man.

Genesis 2:7 says, *"And the LORD God formed man of the dust of the ground, and breathed into his nostrils the breath of life; and man became a living being."* Whatever God wants, He gets. God doesn't do anything haphazardly or by accident. The first earthly being God created with a soul was man. God made man first, and whatever He puts first is a foundation. Then came Eve, and after that came the children in due order.

God has rested everything on man. Any foundation must be strong enough to handle the structure that will be built on it afterward. When you want to find out what the problems are in the community or in the nation, you will end up where God started—with man. If you want to fix the problems, you start with man and work your way back.

Every man reading these words is under pressure and stress. If you are at the breaking point, I can assure you that the only reason you are about to break is because somewhere, in some way, you are not doing things the way God has ordained. It sounds tough and unfair, but the fact is that you are a foundation. Therefore, since God doesn't make mistakes, you, as the foundation that God laid down, can support and shoulder whatever burden God allows to be laid on you. He will give you the grace and strength to handle everything He has ordained.

> *God gives strength to handle everything He has ordained.*

## Stand on the Rock of Salvation

If you take on something God never told you to do, or if you decide to do something your way instead of His way, then you are in danger of breaking under a load that isn't yours. God didn't make man the foundation because man is superior to woman; they are not. He made man the foundation because He wanted to, and He never expected man to stand in their human strength. God expects man to stand on the spiritual strength of the Rock of salvation, the Son of God.

Women have an equally high calling, value, and anointing from God. Yet in God's order their chief function in life, in the marriage relationship, and in the home is different from man's function. God went to the ground to make man, but He went to the man to make woman.

Have you ever noticed that men generally look attractive even when they are dirty? Even the well-researched and expensive commercials on television have no problem showing a man who is sweaty and dirty on the job getting flirty glances from a well-dressed woman. Women, for some reason, just don't look as attractive when they are dirty. That is because the woman wasn't pulled out of the ground; she was pulled out of man.

God covered man, pulled the woman out of man, and took the child out of the woman. Now He expects the man to cover the woman and the child. Whatever God took out of man and put in woman, He never put back. That is why we continue to seek each other out to find what we don't have.

> *God expects man to stand on the strength of the Rock of salvation.*

Man and woman are divided in function but equal in essence. God made the woman to be a wife and a mother. Her body is uniquely equipped with the organs, bone structure, and complex hormonal systems necessary to conceive, carry, bear, and nurture children.

The medical profession decided they knew better than God in the 1950s and 1960s when they announced that it was old-fashioned and second-best for new mothers to nurse their babies. But God's way has finally prevailed, and the natural way of nursing babies is back. Although I am thankful for baby formula in cases where nursing is impossible or difficult at best, the use of formula was promoted as a way that was better than God's way. Yet, God's way prevailed.

Just because women are made to be able to have children, fathers have an important role to play as well. They give their children purpose and identity. Boys get their identities from their fathers. Girls also form their identities based on their fathers' affirmation (or lack thereof). Every child's makeup starts with both parents operating in their roles in the home.

Psalm 127:1 says, *"Unless the LORD builds the house, they labor in vain who build it."* The psalmist went on to say:

> *Behold, children are a heritage from the Lord, the fruit of the womb is a reward. Like arrows in the hand of a warrior, so are the children of one's youth. Happy is the man who has his quiver full of them; they shall not be ashamed, but shall speak with their enemies in the gate.* (verses 3–5)

## Aborting Our Future

Children are God's arrows in our hands, and it is our responsibility and privilege to launch them into the future equipped with all of the accumulated knowledge, wisdom, wealth, and power

> *Children are God's arrows in our hands.*

that we have gained and that our forefathers have left us. Our problem is that we are constantly "aborting" our future generations through present-day ignorance and disorder.

I am the son of a preacher, but the only reason I am here is because my mother understood the Scriptures and had the strength of conviction and character to submit to my father—even when he didn't deserve it. When she married him, he hid two secrets from her: He was an alcoholic; and he really wasn't saved. Mom discovered the truth after she married Dad, but because she was married to him, she submitted to him and respected him anyway.

Mom would get up in the morning and cook breakfast from scratch—the old-fashioned way. If Daddy came home at eleven o'clock or midnight, she would get out of bed and fix him a plate of food. Then she would sit there until he was finished, wash the dishes, and have his clothes ready for the next day.

## An Arrow Shot Into the Next Generation

It wasn't easy for my mother to submit to and respect my alcoholic father in the early days, but she had an unshakable conviction that God's Word was true, and she lived according to her conviction. I thank God that my mother was a godly woman with the faith to stand when everything around her told her to run.

I can remember the day that she almost left. She had just about had enough, and she started packing her things. I was crying my heart out in the bathroom, and finally I went to her because I knew my daddy was being a stubborn fool. I said, "Mama, if you leave, I'll die." And she said, "I ain't going nowhere." Because my godly mother was willing to cover me, I'm here fulfilling my divine call today. In time, my father became the man that God called him to be and that my mother believed he could become.

My daddy's call was to start churches. I never remember Daddy pastoring one church for more than three years. He would go in and pioneer a church, build a nice building, and then leave. Guess what? That same pioneering legacy is going on today in my ministry, but to an even greater degree.

I was an arrow that was shot into the next generation. God is bringing pastors to me from all over this country who are laying down their ordination certificates and saying, "I am submitting to you, Bishop, and I am bringing my church under the authority of this church." I tell you that this leadership mantle and calling was birthed first in my daddy, the called-out builder of churches. In my generation, God is submitting under this authority churches that are already built.

Whether male or female, we need to understand that all of the problems we fill our days with—marital, childrearing, financial, or relational—are distractions and smoke screens that the devil is using to keep our eyes off what God has ordained for us to do. As members of the body of Christ, we have been drawn away to little battles in our backyards, but we are losing the fight to fulfill our divine destinies in God. We are fighting the battles of our own choosing, not realizing we are passing up a far greater treasure by losing the war of obedience to God's will and Word.

One of our most serious problems is that we have trained the congregations in the body of Christ to be spiritually self-ish. We come to church services with the primary goal of enjoying ourselves and being blessed. It is good to be blessed, but God has a higher purpose and priority for our lives than to be blessing-seekers all of our days. Our inward focus on personal blessings for "us four and no more" has caused us to miss what God is doing in the earth today. We are not saying to the Lord, "Your will be done." We are saying, "My will be done, and with as little trouble as possible please, Lord." We don't understand that the only reason God blesses us is so that we can be a blessing!

The Bible doesn't tell us, "Present your requests to God so you can avoid all sacrifice, which is unreasonable service anyway." No, the apostle Paul said, *"I beseech you therefore, brethren, by the mercies of God, that you present your bodies a living sacrifice, holy, acceptable to God, which is your reasonable service"* (Romans 12:1).

> ## The only reason God blesses us is so that we can be a blessing!

### CONFORMED TO THE IMAGE OF CHRIST

Many sincere Christians claim they are "suffering for Christ," but most of our "suffering" comes in one of two ways. We "suffer" because of our uncontrolled flesh, our desires, or our lack of discipline. We also "suffer" when we are in the middle of God's maturation process and are being conformed to Christ's image. The first kind of suffering isn't suffering at all; it is a warning to shape up, make right choices, and tell the flesh no. The second kind of suffering is actually the mercy of God at work in us. If we allow patience to have *"its perfect work,"* as in the words of the apostle James, we will *"be perfect and complete, lacking nothing"* (James 1:4).

According to Ephesians 6, a fight is going on that we do not understand or even perceive in many cases. God wants to manifest His power through the church in this fight, and that is why it is so important for the church to get in the order of God. God's order strengthens the church and everything it touches. As the families are strengthened, the local church is strengthened, and the power of God can be manifested through the corporate body.

We are a body of many different members united under one Head. It is vital that we find our place and function without envy or strife so we can all receive God's blessing and fulfill our destiny. If you have ever stubbed your little toe or broken a finger, you know how your whole body is affected when even one of your smallest and least noticed members is hurt or out of place. Things get even more serious when major organs or weight-bearing parts are out of place or missing.

## THE MAN OF THE HOUSE

I believe you can trace every major problem affecting the church and society today to the man of the house. When the man shirks his God-given responsibilities in relationships, marriage, or the home, all hell literally breaks loose. Something else will quickly step in to fill the void a man's absence creates. Once the man steps back into God's order, everything else gets stronger.

You bring the measure of God's power that is manifested in your home to the local church. When you have nothing at home, you bring all of that nothingness to the church. So Christians are disappointed when they bring all of their nothingness together and expect something big to happen.

Why is it that nine out of every ten churches in this country don't even impact the single block of property their building occupies? They are out of the order of God. Therefore, the power of God is missing from the homes and lives of their people—individually and corporately. We can never have God's power unless we come into agreement with one another and come into God's order at home and at church.

When we come together in God's order under the influence of the same indwelling Spirit of God, we will see the kingdom of God take over through a manifestation of the power of God on a level we have never seen before. On the other hand, the churches that manage to have a wonderful time without the Spirit of God on Sundays and Wednesdays get only what they can produce in the flesh. Any church that operates outside of God's order is functioning in man's power; it has no power to influence and impact the world around it. This kind of church will find itself overcome by a society like the one described by the apostle Paul in his second letter to Timothy:

> *But know this, that in the last days perilous times will come: for men will be lovers of themselves, lovers of money, boasters, proud, blasphemers, disobedient to parents, unthankful, unholy, unloving, unforgiving, slanderers, without self-control, brutal, despisers of good, traitors, headstrong, haughty, lovers of pleasure rather than lovers of God, having a form of godliness but denying its power. And from such people turn away!* (2 Timothy 3:1–5)

This sounds like the news stories we hear year after year describing the stars in the typical professional sports draft, doesn't it? This could be the personal biography of America's favorite musicians and movie stars, or even worse, a description of the elders' kids in your own church! What is happening to us? A quick survey tells us we have skyrocketing preteen pregnancies, free condom distribution in public schools, drive-by shootings, child pornography in print and on the Internet, abortion on demand, and assisted suicide. We also have rampant child abuse, near-total family breakdown, and murder without a second thought.

Judges 17:6 says, *"In those days there was no king in Israel; everyone did what was right in his own eyes."* This plague has moved into the church. For instance, the leadership that was at New Birth when I arrived openly disregarded the ministry gift God had set in the body according to Ephesians 4:11–14, until God changed the order of things. Anytime we choose to *"do what* [is] *right in* [our] *own eyes"* regardless of what the Scriptures say, we have committed a sin that can poison every area of our lives.

## BENEFITS AND BLESSINGS

When I committed my life, ministry, and our church to living in God's order instead of man's, the New Birth church family became debt-free a little over a year later. God made one hundred seventy acres of prime property available to us adjacent to the Atlanta airport. The land was worth over ten million dollars, but the man who owned it was mad at his son, so he offered it to us for three million dollars.

I went to the bank and said, "We need three million dollars." The bankers looked at me and said, "Sir, we don't make those kinds of loans." I just smiled and said, "You'll make it.

Just call me." The next day they called me, and we bought the land.

We held the property for fourteen months; then we sold it for fourteen million dollars, clearing eleven million dollars on the transaction after paying off our loan. We bought two hundred forty acres just up the street from our present location, paid off all of our bills, and put two million dollars in the bank. God did all of that, and we didn't even touch any of our tithes and offerings.

We have a fitness club and a five-acre park, and a tennis court was given to us. God has given us incredible favor—even our families will tell you that they have been blessed ever since we put our house in order.

That is the challenge the church in America faces in this hour. Once we get our homes, individually and corporately, in God's order, He will bless us. Once God's blessing comes, He expects us to stretch beyond our own abilities and resources to do something for Him where His glory is really needed.

> *God stretches us beyond our abilities to show His glory.*

God wants suburban churches to stretch themselves by faith at His direction to sow buildings, land, resources, and people in inner-city neighborhoods in Jesus' name. He wants big city churches to expand their vision and plant churches in rural areas where God's Word is hard to find. God wants to tear down every fence we have labored to build in the flesh over the last two centuries in America. He wants His church

to take the lead by manifesting His glory in interracial rec-
onciliation around the cross of Jesus. He wants the church to
take over neighborhoods currently overtaken by crime, gang
warfare, and ruling poverty spirits. These things will `church
isn't doing anything to change the world. We're content just to
keep going through the motions.

Someone who knows something ought to say something.
We are in a rut, and we are doing things religiously because
that's the way it has always been done. What if it has always
been done that way because no one knew any better? The
church has failed the primary test of God's Word: There is no
fruit being produced. How do we know? Because nothing is
really changing in our families and communities.

You may ask, "Now, Bishop, it isn't all that bad, is it?"
That depends on how many times you want to keep being
delivered from the same thing. Here is a deep truth to keep in
mind: Change is not change until a change is made. God has a
certain way of doing things, and if we reject His way in favor
of our own way, we will reap the fruit of our own labors: no
fruit at all.

I admit that we have to pay a high price for the lasting
benefits of God's process of growth and maturity. But we pay
an even higher price when we refuse them! You may be sitting
there right now with this book in your hands, just floating in
misery because you are stagnant. That is what is happening
to the church.

The church around the world, and in America especially,
is paying a very dear price today because we have looked at
the challenge of change and said, "Oh, that is too expensive.

I think I'll try an easier, quicker route." Because we refused God's challenge to change over the last few decades, we have lost our children and our families, we have given up our neighborhoods and lost our money, and many of us are even losing our minds and health. Yet few, if any, dare to say anything!

## IMPACTING OUR NEIGHBORHOODS

Five or six years ago I did something every pastor and church leader should do on a regular basis. I asked myself, *If this church building were to burn down, would our community notice—aside from the easier traffic flow?* I really had to wrestle with that question then because we were spending most of our time talking about world missions and other distant ministries. While mission outreach is very important, I had to admit that our church hadn't really made an impact on our community. We had failed in our first mission.

> **If your church were to leave, would the community notice?**

One of the kingdom principles we would like to forget is that a man must be faithful in what he has been given before he can expect more. (See 1 Corinthians 4:2.) I realized early in my life that God, in His sovereignty, was directing my steps, and He was orchestrating one divine appointment after another. So, as pastor of New Birth Missionary Baptist Church, God had specifically placed me in that church and that local community to reveal His kingdom. Once that was settled, I knew the mission of the "house." We began to step

92

into line with God's purposes, and we started by putting our own house in order.

The principles and insights I share here are not based on theoretical what-ifs; they are based on things we have proven in the real world. They are the foundation and driving force of God's favor that catapulted us from a church of three hundred to a growing church of twenty-five thousand in less than a decade.

This ministry has boldly carried God's light into inner-city neighborhoods, the criminal court system, public high schools, the Georgia State Senate, the United States Senate, and even into the White House itself. Under God's direction we have challenged antibiblical laws, Supreme Court rulings, state and national legislators, and church leaders with the truth of God's Word. We are under a mandate from God to take the gospel of Jesus into the world without compromise.

Today I can honestly say that metropolitan Atlanta would miss us very much if something caused us to move away or shut down. The New Birth congregation finances and operates vital support programs in the city and pumps large sums of money and thousands of volunteer hours into key areas such as youth offender intervention programs, public school programs, and support and outreach programs for homeless women and children. We are involved in every aspect of life, and we are making a major impact in the Atlanta metropolitan areas.

This, in turn, is causing us to gain major footholds in the city infrastructure. When you are a politician in a major metropolitan area, it isn't wise to dismiss or ignore a highly unified, committed, and motivated group of voters exceeding twenty-five thousand people representing almost every voting precinct in your city. It is even more foolish when a number of the most highly placed political and judicial leaders in the city are deeply committed members and leaders in the church!

From my very first days as a pastor it was clear that the vision God had given me was too large for me to ever accomplish alone. I was in Jonathan's position:

> *Then Jonathan said to the young man who bore his armor, "Come, let us go over to the garrison of these uncircumcised; it may be that the LORD will work for us. For nothing restrains the LORD from saving by many or by few." So his armorbearer said to him, "Do all that is in your heart. Go then; here I am with you, according to your heart...." And Jonathan climbed up on his hands and knees with his armorbearer after him; and they fell before Jonathan. And as he came after him, his armorbearer killed them. That first slaughter which Jonathan and his armorbearer made was about twenty men within about half an acre of land.*
>
> (1 Samuel 14:6–7; 13–14)

## JONATHAN'S ANOINTING

Things were at a standstill until Jonathan received a dose of mountain-moving faith and spoke to the young man who carried his armor. Somehow the anointing upon Jonathan passed into that young man and gave him the courage to do what King Saul and six hundred soldiers would have never done. He agreed unconditionally with Jonathan's impossible vision and marched off with him to take on a whole army!

Jonathan single-handedly knocked twenty people to the ground, but it was his faithful armorbearer who came right behind him and struck the same enemy soldiers with Jonathan's sword and killed them. The bold strike by Jonathan and his armorbearer seems to have triggered an earthquake of fear that put the entire Philistine army on the run. It was only at this point that the disheartened King Saul and the rest of the Israelite army joined in the rout of the enemy. (See 1 Samuel 14:15–20.)

### CAPTURING THE SPIRIT OF A LEADER

The problems in the body of Christ and in the kingdom are the inability and the unwillingness of believers to give their hearts to or to capture the spirit of the leader. Doing so seems to be giving that leader too much power. So, folks say, "I'm not going that far." Worse yet, they walk away criticizing others who give their heart to the house of God, calling them puppets.

Such individuals have not read the Scriptures. Jesus came and could have been equal with God. But He submitted himself, even to the death on a cross. (See Philippians 2:8.) He did not come to do His own thing. We have too many people who have come to church and to the kingdom with their own agendas. They are trying to carve out their own congregations within the congregation.

Please don't be deceived. Just because you are sitting in the midst of a group of people who are in agreement with you doesn't mean that God agrees. When the service is over you may huddle together and give your opinion about what the pastor said in his sermon. Or perhaps they all look to you to see if you nod in approval of the pastor's message because they won't believe the message unless you give it your "okay." Such folk are not submitted to the headship of the pastor over the house—the shepherd of the church flock. They are submitted to you, and you are causing division in the house. That division hinders your friends from receiving the generational transfer God intends for them to have.

Matthew 23:11–13 describes this attitude:

*But he who is greatest among you shall be your servant. And whoever exalts himself will be humbled, and he who humbles himself will be exalted. But woe to you, scribes and Pharisees, hypocrites! For you shut up the kingdom of heaven against men; for you neither go in yourselves, nor do you allow those who are entering to go in.*

If you are one who stands in the way, hindering and sabotaging another's generational transference by seeding rebellion into their minds, you are no better than the Pharisees. They did the same thing. You may be satisfied with church as usual with no manifestation of God's presence, but the truth is the world is hurtling toward hell.

> *Elisha received a double anointing because of his attitude.*

Your attitude in this matter of transference is vitally important. Realize that Elisha was not the only spiritual apprentice to Elijah, but he was the only one who caught the double portion of his spirit. What made the difference was his *attitude*. Even when Elijah seemed to be rejecting him, walking away from him, trying to get rid of him, Elisha held steady. Three times, Elijah turned to him and said, *"Stay here, please, for the* LORD *has sent me on to Bethel"* (2 Kings 2:2, 4, 6). Those words probably cut Elisha deeply, but he never left Elijah, was never offended, never got angry, never walked off.

Too many church members are easily offended with leaders, walking off when they feel unnoticed or overlooked. Is that you? Are you easily offended by a leader who overlooks your gift or seems to neglect your presence? If so, you must realize what God's purpose is for your attending that particular church. God may have placed you in that congregation to catch something He has placed into the spirit of your leader. You may not be there to be noticed, so seek God and don't miss your spiritual inheritance. Elisha didn't, but all the other spiritual apprentices did miss it. Only one caught the anointing. In your generation, I hope one will be you.

The most important thing for you to do is pray. If you remain in prayer, you won't miss your destiny, and you won't be seduced by those who are being used by the enemy to distract you. You know, Elisha had many opportunities to be distracted also. But he kept his eyes on the prize and was granted dominion in his generation.

## A Submissive Heart

We saw in Malachi 4:6 that God said He would turn the *"hearts of the fathers to their children and the hearts of the children to their fathers."* As we mention, this is a matter of the heart. But it doesn't just concern love and obedience. Another key element is submission.

David was given a vision by God to build a temple. But he was not permitted to actually build it. The vision was for his son Solomon. The son was able to build what the father saw, which suggests he caught the spirit and heart of this father. (See 1 Chronicles 28.)

What we are starting in our generation may be destined to be completed in the next generation. Not all of your vision will be manifested in your lifetime. The vision of the Lord is so great that it often requires several generations to fulfill the call. You may feel overwhelmed by the vision and calling of God on your life. Realize that God may be sending youngsters to catch your heart and pick up your mantle.

You young people, study your bloodline and ask God if your mother or father started something that He is expecting you to finish. If so, grab a hold of that vision instead of trying to start something new.

Sadly for Solomon, his own sons never caught his vision the way he had originally caught his father David's vision. Equally sad, his own sons never captured his heart.

Ecclesiastes 6:1–2 says:

*There is an evil which I have seen under the sun, and it is common among men: a man to whom God has given riches and wealth and honor, so he lacks nothing for himself of all he desires; yet God does not give him power to eat of it, but a foreigner consumes it.*

Solomon called this *"vanity"* and an *"evil affliction."* Solomon caught the heart of his father and built the temple for which David raised money. But because his own sons didn't catch his vision, all his wealth, power, and dominion went to strangers.

The same is going on in today's world. You may wonder, "Why am I broke while others seem to have so much?" It may be that you didn't receive a generational transfer that God intended for you. Therefore God said, "I won't let you eat it. Foreigners will enjoy it."

If you believe God has placed you in your church, then it's vitally important that you learn to submit to the leadership under which He's placed you. You must receive what God has placed within them in order to receive these benefits for yourself. Doing so is a part of your submission to Him. If you cannot submit to leadership, you may discover that neither can you submit to God. The problem lies within your own heart.

## RECEIVING YOUR LEADERS

If you examine God's Word from cover to cover, you will see that time and again God uses men and women to accomplish His will. We like to think that since we have all been made kings and priests in Christ, we don't

> *Time and again, God uses men and women to accomplish His will.*

need leaders anymore. That really isn't up for debate.

The apostle Paul clearly stated, *"But now God has set the members, each one of them, in the body just as He pleased"* (1 Corinthians 12:18). The context of this statement makes it clear that Paul was answering complaints and concerns about the

99

gifts and leadership rank in the local church. The Bible also commands us to obey those in authority over us, including our church leaders, even though none of them are perfect. (See Romans 13:1–3.)

The book of Hebrews tells us to *"obey those who rule over you, and be submissive, for they watch out for your souls, as those who must give account. Let them do so with joy and not with grief, for that would be unprofitable for you"* (Hebrews 13:17). The church is not meant to be ruled by majority vote.

Many people have a serious problem when someone tells them to obey human leaders. They point to all of the leaders who have misused and abused their authority and trust, and I admit that these things happen. I am certainly not advocating that you stay in a church with a pastor who abuses his power. The shepherd should watch out for the sheep. However, we need to realize that if we don't submit, we aren't covered spiritually. Even Jesus submitted to the Father.

David was a man after God's own heart, but there is no way he could be called perfect. David's life history revealed that he was a liar, an adulterer, a cold-blooded murderer, a widely feared professional soldier, and a lousy father. Yet God chose him to lead Israel, and specifically chose to send us Jesus Christ through David's lineage.

## A Blessing and a Curse

The very last prophetic words God uttered in the Old Testament through Malachi were, *"Lest I come and strike the earth with a curse"* (Malachi 4:6). The curse was promised if the hearts of the people didn't turn.

This world is already under a curse. It is evident in our downward spiraling statistics concerning divorce, abortion, incest, rape, violence, corruption, and scandal (even in the church). The greatest indictment of all is that, in most cases, you can't tell the Christians apart from the non-Christians— we're all alike. We got what we asked for.

Two people in the Old Testament perfectly depict the nature of this curse, and they were both members of the house of David: Solomon and Absalom. Later in his life, Solomon became a bitter man because, despite all of his wisdom, he failed to prepare for the future:

> Then I hated all my labor in which I had toiled under the sun, because I must leave it to the man who will come after me. And who knows whether he will be wise or a fool? Yet he will rule over all my labor in which I toiled and in which I have shown myself wise under the sun. This also is vanity. Therefore I turned my heart and despaired of all the labor in which I had toiled under the sun. For there is a man whose labor is with wisdom, knowledge, and skill; yet he must leave his heritage to a man who has not labored for it. This also is vanity and a great evil. (Ecclesiastes 2:18–21)

According to God, if you have not prepared someone to take your heart by inheritance, you have raised children (either natural or spiritual) in vain. Solomon was the wisest man who ever lived—even Jesus attested to that. He was the world's wisest and richest man, yet at the end of his life he said, "Everything is vanity because I have to leave everything that I have to my children who don't have my heart. They may lose what I have acquired."

## The Curse Stops Right Here

We should be preparing a generation for the future, or we will reach the sunset of our lives and find that everything we have done has been in vain. Too many of us are stranded arrows who were forced to start all over. "My grandma was broke, my mama was broke, and so am I. My grandma got divorced, my mama got divorced, and so did I." Wait! Somehow, somewhere, somebody in the bloodline has to stand up in Christ and say, "Enough is enough. The curse stops right here, and right here is where God's blessing begins!"

Most of us in the body of Christ are losing ground because we don't understand that God goes from faith to faith and from glory to glory. (See Romans 1:17; 2 Corinthians 3:18.) We can sing about it, but we can't walk in it. We can shout about it, but we can't live it.

God doesn't want us to start over in every generation. He wants to build family line upon family line, from generation to generation. This goes for your family, and it applies to the family of God as well. Anytime we try to take a shortcut or find an easier way, we cut ourselves off from God's blessing and inherit the curse of Absalom.

## The Curse of Absalom

Absalom was one of David's greatest sons. He seemed to possess more natural leadership ability than Solomon. If Absalom hadn't been so rebellious, he might have been the one chosen to do what Solomon eventually did. Absalom had so much charisma, confidence, and power that he was able to turn most of the nation against his father, King David. Now that man was powerful! But instead of inheriting his father's heart, Absalom chose to envy his father's position and power. Eventually he nearly succeeded in wrenching his father's throne away from him, but in the end he died a rebel's death, suspended between heaven and earth.

> *Now Absalom in his lifetime had taken and set up a pillar for himself, which is in the King's Valley. For he said, "I have no son to keep my name in remembrance." He called the pillar after his own name. And to this day it is called Absalom's Monument.*     (2 Samuel 18:18)

Absalom was childless. His life was barren spiritually, physically, and historically. The only monument he left behind was a shameful legacy of betrayal and rebellion that ended in his untimely death. Absalom cut himself off from his father and failed to train up a son, so he also failed to give anybody the ability to inherit his heart. Absalom was forced to name some-

> *I have been given a name to use, and that is the name of Jesus.*

thing after himself, and he put it in a valley where, ironically, it became a lasting monument to his senseless rebellion rather than to his wisdom or power.

When we have to start all over because there is no inheritance or generational transfer of the heart, we are forced constantly to put our names on things in the vain hope that somebody will remember us after we are gone. I've settled the question. My success doesn't have anything to do with making a name for myself. I have been given a name to use, and that name is Jesus. As for sons, I am a wealthy man. I have a church full of sons and daughters, and I have been blessed with many children in my own house as well.

I have even named my successor to carry on the vision at New Birth Missionary Baptist Church should I leave my assignment early. When I die, if Jesus tarries, my successor will take up the reins and will have the same spirit and the same vision I have, yet he will be expected to take the people to another level. That is the secret of the inheritance of the heart. We see it in the way Jesus transferred to us His calling, His anointing, and His Spirit. He expects us to take what He gave us to another level. Jesus gave us a perfect picture of the ultimate inheritance of the heart when He said:

> *Most assuredly, I say to you, he who believes in Me, the works that I do he will do also; and greater works than these he will do, because I go to My Father. And whatever you ask in My name, that I will do, that the Father may be glorified in the Son.* (John 14:12–13)

I am not here just to play around. When I die, the devil will still have to contend with my great-grandchildren, who will be better off than I was in the spirit realm. So if I am giving the devil a little bit of trouble today, then by the time he gets to my great-great-granddaughter, he is really going to tremble.

## THE LOSS OF INHERITANCE IS A CURSE

Absalom's curse is the same curse that is described in Malachi 4:6. When a son fails to turn his heart toward his father, or when a father fails to turn his heart toward his son, a curse descends upon them. This curse is affecting all of us in the body of Christ because it is the failure of a parent to understand and honor the importance of the inheritance of the saints.

The Absalom curse needs to be destroyed, but that poses a problem for "instantaneous saints" because it isn't going to be destroyed in one day or even in one generation. We can begin the process of its destruction today, but since we have allowed the curse to reach flood stage over hundreds of generations, it will take a farsighted people who are willing to go to the flood plain at the Jordan and die one more time. The cure for a generational curse is a godly generational transfer, a transgenerational inheritance of the heart.

Our God is a God of generations. That is why He calls Himself the God of Abraham, Isaac, and Jacob. He is not giving himself a title, but providing a description of himself. He is saying, "Everything I do is generational. But you've got to catch the heart and the spirit of what I'm doing, and the heart and the spirit of the father with whom I am leading you."

> *Our God is a God of generations: the God of Abraham, Isaac, and Jacob.*

The most deadly aspect of Absalom's curse is that it limits every generation to a single lifetime of work, and it stops anyone from being able to pick up what those before them learned or accomplished. Negative aspects of the curse, such as physical and spiritual disease, disabilities, and chronic debilitating sins, pass through the bloodline. David's problem with adultery and extreme sexual appetites was passed on to several of his descendants, including Solomon. But Solomon also seems to have inherited his father's heart for God's house.

### Your Own Vision or God's Vision?

The Absalom spirit confounds the church with this seemingly spiritual idea that people must find their own vision. On the surface, this statement sounds solid and biblical. We like to rephrase it and tell other people, "We must find the desire for originality and creativity. We must demand our rights. I have a right to get my own vision."

Jesus, on the other hand, took the totally opposite approach:

> *Then Jesus answered and said to them, "Most assuredly, I say to you, the Son can do nothing of Himself, but what He sees the Father do; for whatever He does, the Son also does in like manner. For the Father loves the Son, and shows Him all things that He Himself does; and He will show Him greater works than these, that you may marvel. For as the Father raises the dead and gives life to them, even so the Son gives life to whom He will. For the Father judges no one, but has committed all judgment to the Son, that all should honor the Son just as they honor the Father. He who does not honor the Son does not honor the Father who sent Him."* (John 5:19–23)

Hear me out, because I am not saying, "Don't be creative." I am saying, "Don't be creative first and then check with God.

Get God's instruction first, and then release your creativity." Many times we use creativity as a substitute for God.

This also applies to the business world. Most Christian business people try to be creative to sell more. Holy Spirit entrepreneurs, on the other hand, first ask themselves, "Why did God set me up in business? What is God's purpose, and what does the Lord intend for me to do through my business?" Once you know the answers to these questions, you can be truly creative. I guarantee you that whenever you find your divine purpose and operate in what God established, you don't have to be as creative, because He has already created the market and lined up your customers. He has already provided the way for each of us, but we usurp the way of God because we try to be marketers instead of sons led by the Spirit of God. (See Romans 8:14.)

The same principle applies to our marriages, our family lives, and our ministries. Don't try to save these things; return to the reason or cause that created them in the first place. Once you have an idea why God put you together with your wife and gave the two of you your teenage son, the problems are well on their way to being worked out.

## WHAT IS DADDY DOING?

Jesus said, "I cannot do anything that I don't see My Father doing." Our children should be saying the same thing and operating the same way. "I don't do a thing that I don't see Daddy doing." This is true government, but we don't have it in our homes. That is why our children cannot stand authority. The attitude Jesus had toward His Father and the way He conducted Himself is the prime example of the next generation taking God's purposes to an even higher level.

Jesus took this to what most of us think is an extreme level when He said, *"I can of Myself do **nothing**. As I hear, I judge; and My judgment is righteous, because I do not seek My own will but the will of the Father who sent Me"* (John 5:30, emphasis added). Jesus was saying, "I don't have the authority to do anything. I don't seek after My own will. I don't run on My own initiative."

## GET THE HEART FROM THE HEAD

I tell the members of my congregation, "You are sons and daughters in the church, and I am father." I don't do this because I'm an egomaniac; I do it because it is biblical. A lot of people don't want to deal with that, but it's in the Bible:

> *Obey those who rule over you, and be submissive, for they watch out for your souls, as those who must give account. Let them do so with joy and not with grief, for that would be unprofitable for you.* (Hebrews 13:17)

When I first took this stand on biblical order in the church, I heard it all: "It sounds like we're giving somebody too much power." "It sounds cultic." "Sounds like a controlling spirit to me." "Aren't we just giving in to the sovereignty of God a bit much here? Where is our free will?" "I can't go with that. I love to read about Saul, David, and Moses and the three and a half million Israelites who followed him. Sure, they were obedient some of the time, but I can't do that because I've got a vision. I've got something that the Lord told me."

These excuses and complaints highlight one of the most dangerous areas in any church setting. The Absalom spirit delights in repeating its favorite theme—pitting young leadership against old leadership in the church. The younger leadership does not understand that they have to get the heart of the spiritual headship to prosper.

Jesus, the Head of the church, the senior Shepherd, plants His vision for a church body in the local undershepherd of that church. It is this vision, dwelling in the heart of His chosen leader, which is destined to go from generation to generation. But such a vision can only go on when it is passed along in godly order from one generation to the next as they all work together to see God's dream come to pass.

If God gave you a vision, then you should know that whatever God spoke to you, you cannot accomplish in one lifetime. If you can, it isn't a vision from God. It is a task or a short-term mission. True visions are transgenerational. This may explain why you thought you were crazy. You were trying to figure out how you were going to get all this done

> *If God gave you a vision, you cannot accomplish it in one lifetime.*

before you died, but now you know the vision was never meant to be accomplished in your lifetime alone. You were intended to start it and then pass along the vision of your heart to someone else at God's direction. Name your successor. Give him your heart. Let him understand that he does not have a vision; he is carrying out something from God that you already started.

### FORTY-YEAR ABORTIONS

Even Satan understands the power of generational transfer. Everything the devil learned in one generation he carefully passed on to the next generation of foolish humans. He keeps on acquiring greater darkness and greater numbers of converts, while the Christians keep aborting their visions after forty years, forcing the next generation to enter the war of the Spirit essentially unprepared and unequipped because they have to keep starting all over. In all of the generations since the day of Pentecost in Jerusalem, generation after generation, the church has not changed much at all—unless you measure our incredible lack of power, integrity, miracles, and unity.

The bottom line is this: God wants you to get His heart so you can pass it on to your children. When you talk to your children (both spiritual and natural) about your experiences in Christ, don't paint candy-coated pictures of how you came from *there* to *here*. The only way you can give God all of the glory is to tell the bad side of the story, too.

Don't try to make them think you were a virgin when you know what happened in the back seat of a Volkswagen and what it did to you. Tell them it wasn't worth it! Tell them the truth! Tell them what you have been through so they won't have to suffer the same pain needlessly. Tell them what your grandma knew, and then explain to them how God has moved and what you have learned in the process. Then watch them, because they need help.

Don't let your living and your mistakes be in vain. Your children—both your natural children and your spiritual children in the body of Christ—are supposed to be better off than you, but that will only come with a deep understanding of how you got *here* from *there*.

People—even our children—can relate better to those who are transparent about their failures and shortcomings. We should allow our brokenness and our scars to become a visible testimony to God's power and willingness to deliver and transform us. God delights in using broken people to bring wholeness and deliverance to others.

He chose David although he was an adulterer and murderer. He chose Moses to confront Pharaoh although he was a murderer with a serious speech impediment. He chose Paul although he was a highly trained Pharisee and one of the most dedicated persecutors of the early church. The problem with church folk is that too many of us are looking for another Jesus in the pulpit. I am quick to let my people in on a secret: I am not He!

### You Can't Drive the Bus without Keys

Your church will never be what God called it to be if the believers who are in their forties step aside without having transferred their heart to the next generation. Many great churches and mighty works in cities across this nation are struggling just to survive today. Why? Because when the original founders or fathers of the church passed on they failed to pass on their vision, heart, and authority to a successor. A good and godly pastor may be struggling to maintain the pastorate, but if the "daddy" God set in place forty years earlier failed to pass along his mantle and heart to this new pastor, the new leader may be trying to drive the bus without keys, gas, or a road map.

In times of need, God will send ordinary men endued with extraordinary vision. If Christ tarries, their vision will be too great for them to accomplish on their own or even in one lifetime. God wants us to honor His sovereignty and trust His ability to use ordinary flawed men as leaders.

Finally, understand that when God sends such leaders into a generation, He doesn't expect those leaders to accomplish His will when they are stuck with hundreds of lone rangers who each think they possess a vision of equal importance to the leader's vision. This takes us back to the *too many cooks spoil the broth* syndrome. Paul made it clear that we don't choose what body part we are to be in the church; it is God who sets us in place as it pleases Him. (See 1 Corinthians 12:14–18.)

> *In times of need, God sends ordinary men with extraordinary vision.*

The greatest testimony of New Birth Missionary Baptist Church will come after I am dead. This church is supposed to soar and accomplish even greater things tomorrow than what we have accomplished today, and it will be because more than twenty-five thousand grains of wheat fell to the ground and died to their own visions and took up the vision of God as their own. Everything I've learned and experienced says that God delivers His vision for local churches and ministries through the set ministry gift He placed at the head.

## A Spiritual Father Shoots You
## into the Future

Paul spoke forcefully about the existence and importance of spiritual fathers in his first letter to the Corinthians. In fact, Paul's ministry lived on well past his lifetime because of his spiritual sons:

> *For though you might have ten thousand instructors in Christ, yet you do not have many fathers; for in Christ Jesus I have begotten you through the gospel. Therefore I urge you, imitate me. For this reason I have sent Timothy to you, who is my beloved and faithful son in the Lord, who will remind you of my ways in Christ, as I teach everywhere in every church.* (1 Corinthians 4:15-17)

A father is one whom God sovereignly chooses to pass on his heart and spiritual legacy to you as a divine inheritance for the future. A father shoots you into the future as an arrow of God's anointing, power, and purpose bearing the accumulated obedience of many generations in your heart.

I am a firm believer in the priesthood of all believers and in the finished work of Jesus Christ on the cross. No man can save us, but it is God's choice that a man should lead us—and God doesn't ask our opinion about the man ahead of time. It takes an even greater trust and faith in God to submit to human leaders when we know they are flawed just as we are. Yet in the end it all boils down to one question: Is God really God, or isn't He?

God is saying to us individually, "No more will generation after generation die, but you will go from faith to faith, from glory to glory." Your grandma might have been broke, and you might not have much money, but you are going to raise up another generation that is going to unlock the doors to pay it all off! There is a sound rising of a holy people who are pregnant with purpose. There is a vision in the house of God that is destined to be echoed by the multitude of voices of the many-membered church. Nothing can turn them around. I hear a battle cry of God.

## TAKE IT TO ANOTHER LEVEL

God has given me, as bishop and senior pastor of New Birth, the vision and the ability to knock the enemy down in certain key areas. But the vision He gave me will never come to pass and impact the Atlanta metropolitan community or the world until the army of armorbearers that God assigned to New Birth rises up with swords in hand. As the people of God rise to the

> *As you respond to the vision, other leaders and churches will rise up.*

challenge, other leaders and churches will rise up with new courage and vision as well. We have already seen this come to pass to some extent, but we are determined to take it to a new level.

One of the greatest challenges in the body of Christ today is our critical shortage of spiritual "daddies." Where are they? Who is taking the time to raise up sons and daughters and really teach them? Who really understands generational succession? I am convinced that every church leader and local congregation that commit to the task of raising up daddies will be empowered and equipped by God to take over and make a lasting difference in their communities. The church filled with anointed spiritual fathers (and therefore mothers as well) would be sorely missed should they leave an area.

## Project Destiny

Even before I started developing spiritual sons who naturally did what they saw "Daddy" do, it was inevitable that our church would make godly waves in our local area, in Atlanta, and later throughout the state of Georgia, and the nation. But it all began with sons.

I've already mentioned my conviction that nearly every major problem in society and the church can be traced back to the man. As a natural extension of this conviction and my passion for youth, the Lord directed me to establish a nonprofit youth diversion ministry called Project Destiny. It began on a small scale when I obeyed the Lord's leading and went to the court system and asked for custody of first-time juvenile offenders who had been convicted of nonviolent crimes. We suggested to the courts that instead of sending these youths to prison, they give them the option of entering Project Destiny.

We knew what the courts also know—the prison system does not work as a rehabilitative system. We also understood that only Jesus Christ and God's Word can permanently change and impact these kids' lives for the kingdom. We noticed that a kid can go into the prison system as a shoplifter and emerge six or twelve months later as a well-trained, big-time bank robber or even a hardened killer.

Our goal was to bring in these young men at risk and tell them that they have destiny. We tell them, "God has you here for a season and a reason. You were born for a purpose, and you were born to be a problem-solver. There is a problem out there that God has created you to solve, and only you can solve it. You are that important to God's kingdom."

Up until that time there were a lot of secular and church-based programs that mentored troubled kids in hope of changing their lives. The problem was that as soon as their time was up with these adult mentors, the kids were sent right back into a hellish household. I knew this had to change, so our program was designed not just for the child but for the whole family. When we offer to take a child out of the court system, we require the parents to participate in the program, too. This includes the counseling sessions, classes, and everything else the program involves. Now we are not only talking about saving a child, we are talking about saving the family—and in turn, saving the generations that will follow.

Everyone in a family being considered for Project Destiny must sign a covenant stating that they understand why they are there and how many meetings they must attend. If they don't want to commit to the covenant, then they can take their chances with the prison system. If they fail to honor the covenant agreement, they understand that the offender will immediately be returned to the custody of the court or the prison system to serve the original sentence. We hold a big celebration at the end of the program for everyone who graduates. So far we have an 89 percent success rate, although we are believing God for a 100 percent success rate.

### GOD'S HEART FOR OUR COMMUNITY

In this program the most common problem we run into is that the parents can't get to New Birth with their child. So we bought two vans specifically for Project Destiny so we could pick up the kids when their parents can't get there. We do what we have to do because it is a priority in the heart of God for our community. Our objective is not to recruit these families as members of New Birth Missionary Baptist Church; it is to teach these families at risk about God's life-changing kingdom principles.

Of course, many of these families do join the church along the way, but our chief goal is to make sure they understand how they fit into God's kingdom. We want them to leave us knowing their divine purpose in God, that they were born for a reason, and that they shouldn't waste their time in this life chasing trivial pursuits.

Many of these families are broken or dysfunctional with only a single parent in the home. However, we are so convinced that both brokenness and healing begin with the man of the house that if the man of the house is missing through divorce, separation, or outright abandonment, we try to find him. Many times we are able to convince these missing fathers to participate in the program as well, sometimes right alongside their ex-wives and the child's stepfather.

The program has become national with the headquarters in Ontario, California. I still serve as chairman of the national advisory board of Project Destiny, and when New Birth donated five hundred thousand dollars as a challenge grant to the project, it made headlines in the Atlanta

*Journal-Constitution* and other newspapers across the country. We are absolutely committed to our youth because they are a major priority with God. This area has dominated our budget almost every year I have been at New Birth, and as a result, we have no shortage of spiritual sons and daughters.

## MARCHING ON

Dr. Martin Luther King Jr. led the march of our fathers and mothers in order to take back the dignity, freedom, liberty, and dominion of his generation. Recently, we took up the torch at his gravesite and carried it once more throughout Atlanta. In so doing, we were proclaiming more than merely the unity and tenacity of our intentions. We were joining our hearts with those gone

> *We will keep the light burning. We will not allow it to be snuffed out.*

before us in time, uniting our purpose with the past and carrying it high in the now.

We will keep the light burning brightly in our generation. We will not allow it to be snuffed out. And, in addition, we will pass it on when our march is completed and our time is done. The light of liberty, morality, truth, and power will not go out. That is our solemn declaration, and we shall not be deterred.

CHAPTER 5

# A CHURCH MANDATE

T he purposes of God are marching through the desert of this darkness into our corporate destiny. When we go forward in step with Him, the dominion of God is revealed in the earth. But far too often this divinely assigned army of destiny falls out of rank and deteriorates into a chaotic mass of confusion as each soldier marches to the beat of his or her own purposes and plans.

God is marching through the earth, but, regretfully, many don't realize that He is marching right past them. While we, as part of the many-member church, bicker and fight among ourselves over every minor point and opinion, we've failed to notice that God has left our fractured groups behind. He is marching on.

Some march on; we are on a mission, pressing on to fulfill our destiny in God's purpose. God Himself is saying, "Enough is enough. The fullness of time is now, and I am ready to reveal Myself as never before."

Where are you? Are you marching forward with God, shining a gospel light into the corruption of this dark age? Or have you been waylaid, distracted, your life preaching a gospel of hypocrisy?

## A Gospel of Hypocrisy

The church today has made the gospel so unrealistic that it has caused more people to stumble and fall than to stand. When I say unrealistic, I am referring to our modern gospel of hypocrisy. The world outside our church walls views Christians as holier-than-thou hypocrites who preach a plastic gospel of "do's and don'ts." The world views us this way because the gospel we preach appears to have nothing to do with the difficult realities of life mixed with the complexities of human weakness. We could use a good dose of honesty in our dealings with non-Christians.

I'm tired of church, and so is God. I'm not tired of worshipping the Lord. I'm not tired of hearing and reading God's Word. I'm not tired of God's people. I'm not tired of witnessing and ministering to the lost and hurting. What makes me tired is the man-made, man-dominated, man-centered facade posing as "the true church."

Jesus Himself defined the true church in the local sense when He said, *"For where two or three are gathered together in My name, I am there in the midst of them"* (Matthew 18:20). However, I've been in many church services where there just wasn't room or time allotted on the agenda for Jesus to be there or have His say.

I have a burning passion to see God right here—in the middle of us—when we gather in His name. Unfortunately, we face a big problem that we haven't yet whipped. A lot of people believe the devil keeps us from seeing God. Others claim that the atmosphere of our age keeps us separated from God's tangible presence. In truth, it's not the devil or any other

120

outside force. Our biggest problem is us! We have made the gospel so complicated with man-made rules, regulations, and hypocrisy that we have hindered the habitation of God.

The best we have seen at this point in church history is just a visitation. I thank God for that, but we need to experience an *overwhelming habitation* of God! The church has been her own worst enemy. Our problems have been perpetuated by ignorance, disobedience, and selfishness and have multiplied from generation to generation.

> ## We need to experience an overwhelming habitation of God.

## MAN APPOINTED LEADERS

The landscape of the American church is littered with man-appointed kings and the shoddy remnants of fractured fleshly kingdoms. We have digressed in our ways all the way back to the days of Israel, when they asked God for a king. The pain we feel is the pain we have brought on ourselves, but there is a better way.

Let me explain. The church today is like the Israelites, who were tired of God's government and His chosen leaders, especially when those leaders failed to produce godly sons to carry God's inheritance into the next generation. The people decided they wanted the more visible leadership of fleshly kings.

*Now it came to pass when Samuel was old that he made his sons judges over Israel. The name of his firstborn was Joel, and the name of his second, Abijah; they were judges in Beersheba. But his sons did not walk in his ways; they turned aside after dishonest gain, took bribes, and perverted justice. Then all the elders of Israel gathered together and came to Samuel at Ramah, and said to him, "Look, you are old, and your sons do not walk in your ways. Now make us a king to judge us like all the nations."*   (1 Samuel 8:1–5)

In the latter part of Samuel's life and ministry as a judge over Israel, the nation's elders had a summit meeting and gave Samuel three reasons for their choice of a king over God's appointed judge: The first reason: "'*You are old,*' and it is time for you to move on." The second: "'*Your sons do not walk in your ways*'; they do not have your heart. You were a good and righteous judge, but the sons you expect to inherit the kingdom have turned away to sin. We don't want any part of them." And the third reason: "We want to be like all the other nations and have kings."

## PAYING THE PRICE

God made it clear that the Israelites were rejecting Him, not Samuel. But Samuel's negligence as a father contributed to the problem. God told Samuel to tell Israel, "Okay, you can have a king. You can have what you want." But He must have reflected, *You would think these people would have learned something with the manna thing in the wilderness.* Samuel obeyed God's instructions and warned the people in advance about the behavior of the king they would choose, but it didn't do any good.

The elders' reply sounds strangely familiar—especially the last part of their answer: "*No, but we will have a king over us, that we also may be like all the nations, and that our king may judge us and go out before us and fight our battles"* (1 Samuel 8:19-20).

The people chose to follow a king, and God gave them Saul. I believe God answered the peoples' request to the letter by choosing Saul according to the criteria of having what "all the other nations had." Saul was tall, dark, and handsome. He was articulate and mighty in looks and deeds.

We shouldn't be amazed when the body of Christ flocks around evangelists and other leaders who look spiritual and regal. Some of these leaders are just as nice on the inside as they are on the outside, but often outward appearance and personal charm have nothing to do with godly character. The problem is that most people don't care, and I'm talking about people in the church as well as nonbelievers. They are too engulfed in the charisma and the exciting events they see unfold under the television lights—the same way Israel was too excited over Saul's selection—to consider what it would mean to them for the painful years ahead.

### After God's Heart

The church is discovering what Israel learned about hastily embracing magnetic leaders who haven't been proven by God's process of maturity. Too often we fail to look at the hearts and lives of our leaders. We need to remember that God rewards us publicly only according to our private lives and deeds.

> *God rewards us publicly according to our private lives and deeds.*

Anybody can put on a show for a little while, but it takes a godly man—whether model material or bald-headed, buff or bow-legged—to walk in holiness and intimacy by spending private time with God day after day. It didn't take Saul very long to expose the true nature of his heart, and the day came when the prophet of God was sent to confront the foolish king of Israel:

> *And Samuel said to Saul, "You have done foolishly. You have not kept the commandment of the LORD your God, which He commanded you. For now the LORD would have established your kingdom over Israel forever. But now your kingdom shall not continue. The LORD has sought for Himself a man after His own heart."* (1 Samuel 13:13–14)

God wanted to establish His kingdom over Israel forever, but it could only be done one way—God's way. God is looking for men and women who are after His heart, and what I am called to say in this chapter is the heart of this book. It may sound revolutionary to some people, but it is God's simple way to build His kingdom—through the inheritance of the heart.

*God's way to build His kingdom is through the inheritance of the heart.*

Saul was forty when he was chosen, and he had everything going for him. Yet from the very beginning he was exposed as a thin-skinned ruler with a hot temper who was given to depression and thoughts of murder. So much for the king the people chose. (I say that the people "chose" Saul because even though Samuel forewarned them about the king's behavior, they chose to have a king anyway. Saul simply lived out Samuel's prophetic warning.) We live in a nation, and may even attend a local church body that is also being led by men and women—man-centered systems of government—whom the people chose.

In stark contrast, David was born ten years after Saul became king, but he represented God's way—God said he was a man after His own heart. I believe we have totally missed or rejected this crucial building block in the body of Christ. God has a sovereign order for the leadership of His flock, and that order is found in the inheritance of the heart. Only that which is centered and set on the heart of God will last.

The church has become the murderer of those who have the heart of God. In other words, we have chosen to cling to government and leadership in our churches that constantly try to bring down and remove the men and methods God has chosen.

## Tickling the Ears of Nursery Saints

Although we are the children of God, we are perishing because of our lack of wisdom. There are a lot of hungry folk out there. I often go to Christian conventions and conferences and find myself preaching something from God's Word that is totally opposite from what everyone else is saying. I believe the church should have graduated long ago from the "bless me" kind of gospel. In the words of the apostle Paul:

*For though by this time you ought to be teachers, you need someone to teach you again the first principles of the oracles of God; and you have come to need milk and not solid food.*

*For everyone who partakes only of milk is unskilled in the word of righteousness, for he is a babe. But solid food belongs to those who are of full age, that is, those who by reason of use have their senses exercised to discern both good and evil.* (Hebrews 5:12–14)

We should be pounding Satan's doors and mending broken bodies and hearts, but we're too busy tickling the ears of the nursery saints. Yet everywhere I go, people are so receptive that I know they are hungry. These people have been hungering for meat for a long time, and for reasons unknown to me, their spiritual fathers and mothers aren't feeding them grown-up food.

The odd thing is that I find almost as many pastors and preachers showing the same hunger. It seems they have been laboring to serve God and His people for years, but they have been pressured to do things "the way they have always been done" or else, when deep down inside them they will tell you, "I hear a different sound." How do I know this? It isn't hard to figure out. It doesn't even take much spiritual discernment. These people give themselves away, because when they hear the truth, their mouths hang open and their eyes become bright with excitement or wet with tears. All they really want is truth.

This nation, together with the whole world, is crying out for truth, but they are not finding it in the place we like to call "the church." As a result, the non-Christian world and many of those attending our churches follow an ever-changing jumble of untruth and lies. Yet there is a call, a voice, an unspoken word that God is whispering into the innermost parts of people around the world. They can't tell you where it comes from or repeat it word for word, but whenever they hear somebody stand up and proclaim it, they lift their heads and feel their hearts beat faster.

One of my dear friends and my spiritual father, Dr. Mark Hanby, once told me, "What would happen if God asked you, 'Why did you do those things I never told you to do?'" That comment had a deep impact on me, and I've discovered that it scares pastors. Why? Because they know that if God never showed up, their church services would still go on just fine without Him. What does that tell you about God's definition versus man's definition of church? For the most part, God isn't showing up in most of America's churches.

## Do You Hear a Different Sound?

I often mention the story of Noah when explaining this "different sound" in the earth. I'm convinced that when Noah loaded up the ark with animals, only certain animals heard the call. God instructed Noah to bring them in two by two, so when Noah went to the nearest pride of lions and called out, all of them didn't come at his command. Most of them glanced his way and then ignored him, but two of them heard the call of destiny and lifted their heads. Perhaps at that same moment all of the animals that were normally prey for the lions also answered that same call.

The different species would be fighting with, fleeing from, or eating one another, as is normal in the order of the earth and the natural food chain. But this time a different order descended on that portion of the planet. There was peace between the species because they were all in the order of God. The future of each species was at stake. Everything flowed according to a higher order to achieve a higher purpose. This is an eternal characteristic of the order of God.

Today, God has raised up certain men and women to proclaim a living word from God for this hour. Everywhere these anointed spokespersons go, they find people who lift their heads, even while engaged in the normal order of things, and say, "I know that voice. I've heard it before." Thousands are being drawn to the Master according to a higher order that often challenges the existing order of man. The existing order that is being challenged most often is the order of man in the institution we have come to call the church. It is time to tear down the foundations of ignorance among God's people so that God is free to be God.

> *We must declare God's living word so that God is free to be God.*

We have a dangerous habit of reading the Bible as if it is a children's storybook. Once you close the cover to a storybook, you go back into the real world. God's Word is not a storybook. It is God's sword, sharp and two-edged for a very good reason: It cuts both ways. Jesus gave us a warning because we need it, and it is time to open the Book again and hear the Word of the Lord:

> [Jesus] *answered and said to them, "Why do you also transgress the commandment of God because of your tradition?...Thus you have made the commandment of God of no*

*effect by your tradition. Hypocrites! Well did Isaiah proph-*
*esy about you, saying: 'These people draw near to Me with*
*their mouth, and honor Me with their lips, but their heart*
*is far from Me. And in vain they worship Me, teaching as*
*doctrines the commandments of men.'"*

(Matthew 15:3, 6–9)

## Presenting a Perverted Gospel

The modern church has managed to present the gospel
in such a perverted way that no one is really willing to
die for it. This isn't the case in China, Pakistan, and countless other areas where persecution against Christians is the
norm. Jesus preached the pure gospel of the kingdom. So did
Peter, Stephen, and the apostle Paul. When they preached the
gospel, people recognized the "different sound" and raised
their heads, thinking, *I finally believe, and there's no other way.*
*I'm ready and willing to die for this. This is why I was born.*

We have watered down the gospel to make it seeker-
friendly. In doing so we have come into "agreement" with
homosexuality, abortion, and countless other immoral issues
about which God's Word is clear; yet we choose to remain
silent and do nothing. In God's eyes we are guilty of "aiding
and abetting" when we remain silent while God says, "Speak
out!"

The church has failed to groom political leaders or do
much of anything to impact her host cities. We're interested
in having church and going home. Therefore, the commitment level of the saints is very low. Yet, the Holy Spirit calls
to hearts, "Let's move out to the streets so we can meet needs.

Let's feed the poor every weekend. Let's plant a church in the heart of the downtown area so we can bring God's light into the darkness." He gets the reply, "Yeah, let's do that. I'll do it if I can just stay in my culture."

We lack the tenacity of our forefathers when they braved public persecution or imprisonment to stand for what they believed. Today, most folk look at the gospel of Jesus Christ as "optional equipment"—just another thing that makes society better. We ministers must accept some of the blame because a lot of the problem is in the presentation. I believe God is angry with us. He said through the prophet Isaiah:

*For My name's sake I will defer My anger, and for My praise I will restrain it from you, so that I do not cut you off. Behold, I have refined you, but not as silver; I have tested you in the furnace of affliction. For My own sake, for My own sake, I will do it; for how should My name be profaned? And I will not give My glory to another.* (Isaiah 48:9–11)

I recently looked into the television cameras that beam our ministry to the nation and around the world and said, "In a lot of churches God is only showing up because of His name. His name is at stake because we've misrepresented it. If He didn't show up, people wouldn't believe He was God."

**We should willingly serve so that God shows up because He is pleased.**

God shouldn't have to show up in our churches just to defend Himself due to our misrepresentation. That is the way of the "church of disorder." We should be so dedicated and willing to serve Him that He shows up just because He's pleased.

How did we get to this state? How is it that we find ourselves not pleasing to God, who is our all in all? To a large extent, it is due to our lack of spiritual maturity. We've refused to get healed from past wounds and move on to the high calling in Christ Jesus. Our immaturity has caused our generations to become weak and barren.

### The Problems Begins at Home

I believe that the destiny of entire local church bodies depends on their willingness to hear this word (from me or from any other godly source) and act on it. This is a very tough word, but I offer no apologies. It is a tough word for men, and it is a liberating word today for women. It is a word of hope for the children and a word of destiny for the family. It is a word of power for the church in an age of confrontation with the powers of darkness. An old Ghanian proverb states, "The ruin of a nation begins in the homes of its people."

The cancer doesn't begin in the White House or in Congress. Why not? The people in those places, and the people who voted them into those offices, all come out of homes. No matter what problem you name or what crime you point out, I guarantee you it came out of the home somehow, some way. Where we are as a nation and where we are as a church was birthed in our homes.

Never having been healed ourselves, we've birthed succeeding generations of children, and we've raised them without growing up ourselves. The results of this systemic immaturity have been disastrous.

I'll never forget the character named Jenny in the movie *Forrest Gump*. The central character, Forrest Gump, was a man who overcame many obstacles to live a wonderful life. Jenny was Forrest's closest childhood friend and the only true love of his life. Yet very few people really remember Jenny's character because they were so keyed in on Forrest. Jenny came from a home of abuse. She was abused by her father, and by the time she was able to run away from home, most of the damage to her life had already been done.

If you focus in on Jenny's character, you will see that throughout the rest of the movie she was trying to work out the pain she endured in her childhood home. Jenny went from abusive relationship to abusive relationship; she was involved in drugs and everything else that came along as she tried to find herself. This pattern of compulsive self-destruction continued until she died an early death after contracting AIDS.

Many of us left home a long time ago, but we are still working through the pain we endured there. We've been praying for deliverance from the hang-ups, the verbal and mental abuse, the physical and sexual abuse, the chronic poverty, or the lack of encouragement and love. All of these things can be traced directly back to our earliest days in the home.

It is in the home that Satan plants time bombs in your spirit that show up only after you say, "I do." These implanted bombs from your parents' unhappy marriage, their fractured personalities, or a relative's twisted sexual appetites will explode with virtually no warning and threaten the very fabric of your own marriage two or three decades later.

Order in a family is important because each generation is to go on to a new and greater glory than the previous generation. God intends for each new generation to build on the foundation and successes of the last generation. If you follow the lineage of Abraham, Isaac, and Jacob, you will see that a spiritual heritage was always being passed on,

> *Each generation is to go on to a new and greater glory.*

and each succeeding generation was ordained to take the authority, blessings, and dominion of that inheritance to a higher place.

Our problem is the disorder of our generations. Due to this chaos, the blessings of spiritual inheritance cease to be passed on to succeeding generations. We poison our seed and doom them to start over.

## ABANDONING OUR CHILDREN

Sometime after the ministry of the original apostles, the church lost the point of evangelism; that error has produced generational weakness and spiritual infertility in the ranks of God's people. Again God says, "Enough is enough!"

If we want a clear picture of the problem, let us look at the statistics of single-parent households in the United States. "How does that tie in to the church missing the point on evangelism, Bishop?" The two are linked at the heart.

God raised up powerful men's ministries like Dr. Edwin Louis Cole's Christian Men's Network, Promise Keepers, and Bishop T. D. Jakes's ManPower to restore true manhood to the church and the nation. Those ministries have run into opposition from feminists, but their goal is to put men back in their homes so they can be faithful husbands, loving fathers, and diligent mentors. The fact that we have an epidemic of men abandoning their wives and children speaks of a much deeper spiritual problem. I have a shocking statement to make: *The church did it first.*

The child abandonment epidemic happened in the spirit realm first. The church has pushed evangelism for more than one hundred years, and the central focus has been to get folks saved. There is only one problem with that. The Lord didn't say, "Go ye into all the world and get folks saved." He said, *"Make disciples"* (Matthew 28:19). The difference between the two is almost as significant as the difference between someone visiting your house and someone moving in permanently as a member of your family.

We refuse to mature the people we lead to Christ, but then we whine and wonder why they become Jehovah's Witnesses the next week, and the following year turn up on the street corner wearing the bow tie and suit uniform of the Nation of Islam. The reason shouldn't be hard to figure out. We had a baby and left him at the altar so we could count our "growth numbers" to see if we beat the First Church down the road.

Ministers brag to one another in sanctimonious tones, "Oh, brother, I had a crusade last week, and do you know that five hundred got saved?" I rejoice over the souls, but I have to ask, "What happened afterward?"

Billy Graham was one of a few evangelists who instituted a system to care for the thousands of spiritual babies won to the Lord in his crusades. He made sure they were contacted by a Bible-believing church that would help them get grounded in the Word and mature in Christ. For the most part, local churches, traveling evangelists, and televangelists have established a reputation of not following up on those saved. They are guilty of conceiving and birthing spiritual babies, only to abandon them at the altar.

I believe God is orchestrating a major shift in leadership and ministry that will astound the minds of the experts. He is telling us, "You are going to either grow up or fall down."

It's time to hear the whole counsel of God for our generation and for the ones to follow. We must determine to grow up or be left behind. The curse of illegitimacy in the church of Jesus Christ must be broken by us.

## God's Mandate

As a church, we are under a mandate from God to take the gospel of Jesus into the world without compromise. This is my compelling personal mandate as well. When I minister at various Bible or church conventions, I often ask, "Aren't you sick of being delivered from the same thing six or seven times? How many meetings are you going to have to attend to find out that some of this stuff we're doing isn't working?" Time and again I've spoken publicly of things that the people were thinking in secret. It galvanizes their thinking, catapulting them into concrete action. This is my mandate from God.

135

I want the church to act as if it is an extension of God here on earth. Too many times in too many churches, we act as if we can't actually let God run His church because He is too unpredictable. "Why, we might miss welcoming the visitors or something."

> *The church is an extension of God here on earth.*

I am out to do more than explain why I say what I say and do what I do. The Lord has given every church leader a mandate to call the church to a higher standard in every realm of life. I am under a burden of God to encourage you, instruct you, push you, and if necessary, offend you in order to move you to take a public stand in the name of Jesus and boldly declare to your world:

**I am here to take over, not to take sides. I have come to take over, and I have no room for compromise.**

This is a whole new way of life, an entirely new way of thinking, a new system of operation. When you get that settled, you're presenting the kingdom.

Now is the time. Yesterday is gone, and tomorrow will be too late. God is coming, and He intends to take over. You and I must take our places now or move aside.

### THE COMING CHURCH

God is bringing forth a new generation of Christians who are fit and ready to run to the battle, whether it is convenient or not. These believers volunteer for the fight, even though they fully understand that the kingdom of God suffers violence, and the violent take it by force. (See Matthew 11:12.) They refuse to be distracted or ruffled by minor nuisances such as traffic problems and opposition from the hesitant saints at First Church around the corner. They are too focused on rebuking the enemy and redeeming the souls of children, prostitutes, and the drug lords who foolishly decided to set up a crack house in God's territory. They sense the time for battle is near, and they are eager to run at the Master's command.

These members of the remnant church heard the rumors long ago; they heard the sounds of God raising up an army, and they were quick to heed His call. No matter where you go, you can find them by the millions saying, "I hear that sound."

I see the princes and kings of this world in the twenty-first century looking to the glorious church because of her glory and power. This church is the head and not the tail. (See Deuteronomy 28:13.) I see the musicians of the world once again copying the music of the church because they are searching for "the sound" that makes the people one. The members of this glorious church will again have a well-earned reputation as "the original creators" because they have learned to tap into the unlimited creativity of the original Creator, their Father. I envision kingdom-controlled businesses, banks, governmental bodies, schools, families, and churches.

Before that great day, God has ordained the birth of millions of sons and daughters of the Spirit into the earth. You see, God has made us pregnant individually as well as corporately. We feel the pangs of labor seizing our souls—God is telling us it is time to be stretched and enlarged.

## What Will It Take?

Sadly, at this point most of us are too overtaken and overrun to make a claim on Satan's territory. I am convinced that the American church in particular will have to go through just a little more pain, but there is a great incentive for us to press through this time of cleansing and preparation. God has made us pregnant with His purpose; and though we are still laboring to deliver God's covering glory to the earth, that day of deliverance is coming! On that day, God's glorious church will be overjoyed, and all of our painful labor will be forgotten when we are overflowing in His glory.

> *Though we still labor, the day of God's deliverance is coming!*

We must be willing to change, to discard the old, to make room for the new. We must lay aside our ways to receive His ways in our hearts. We must expand our houses to take in sons and daughters we never knew existed, and then we must impart our hearts and inheritance to them. We will say to the Lord individually and corporately, *"Be it unto me according to thy Word"* (Luke 1:38 KJV), as a mighty army is born that will share the same heart and vision in Jesus Christ.

New problems call for new solutions. Old problems that haven't been dealt with by old solutions also demand new solutions. Either way you look at it, the church has to change or be left behind because God is on the move.

We have done very little to impact our world over the last two thousand years, in spite of the fact that Jesus finished His work on Calvary and gave us everything we need to succeed in this life. For the most part, we have coasted along on the coattails of those who went before us, especially the church fathers of the first century who were first and second generation spiritual sons of Jesus Christ and the apostles.

It seems that the further we wandered away from the father-son and father-daughter connection instituted by Jesus, the weaker we became. We chose to embrace the agendas and doctrines of men instead of those that God decreed in His Word. We favored programs over personal disciple-ship, political intrigue over personal sacrifice and preferring one another. We consistently chose the easy way rather than the right way because when we counted the cost of obedience to God's vision, we thought the cost was too high.

Today our gospel, our faith, and our witness are so watered down that the American church has become a laughingstock to society and the ranks of darkness alike. Enough is enough. It is time for change.

God is bringing judgment to His house before He brings judgment to the world. His perfect will is to see His bride rise up as a glorious church without spot or wrinkle, a shining light demonstrating His glory to all the world. (See Ephesians 5:27.) However, this picture of the glorious church is dramatically different from the picture of today's church.

### Reject Man-Made Religion

God is out to do more than change our extra-biblical paradigms or ways of thinking. He is out to pull them down and totally destroy them. We've made our own religious ideas and systems into idols that we worship and honor more than God Himself at times. All that is about to come tumbling down. Too often we have tried to build God's house ourselves, or even worse, we've stubbornly chosen to build our church house on a foundation of flesh and place our own name on it. God has a better way, a holier way, and those with ears to hear are hearing a new sound in the earth. It is the sound of God's voice calling, *"Come up here"* (Revelations 4:1).

So then faith comes by hearing, and hearing by the word of God. But I say, have they not heard? Yes indeed: *"Their sound has gone out to all the earth, and their words to the ends of the world"* (Romans 10:18).

I believe the gospel of the Bible must be preached without compromise, but our greatest ministry comes out of brokenness and transparency about our failures and pain. I am convinced that God does not even release us to minister to others until we have been broken and have come through the process with a good attitude (although we usually rush ahead of His timing).

> *Our greatest ministry comes out of brokenness and pain.*

We need to stay the course with God until we are able to stand strong in our brokenness and say, "Let me share with you about the time I made the same mistake in my life and about how God corrected it." I think the major draw of the ministry God has given me at New Birth Missionary Baptist Church is its transparency.

Many times pastors who have fallen into adultery or moral problems will go to other church leaders and confess their sins. They will declare that they have been broken by their experience, and then in the same breath will say, "I want to be restored." Wise church leaders will generally tell them, "You are too strong. The same inner strength that led you to the sin will lead you there again until the day it is totally broken." Very often the "repentant" brothers will fume and complain, saying, "And I came all this way to hear that?" They are still too strong to be truly broken.

I can tell you that the only reason I am still standing in a position of leadership today is that I am willing to admit I am weak. And I have been diligent to train my spiritual sons and leaders to recognize their weaknesses and constantly acknowledge what God has done in their lives. It is my responsibility to be the most transparent leader in the church because I expect it of the leaders under me. Being in touch with the "real" you makes you a better minister.

I am the same man who experienced a broken marriage and a broken heart a number of years ago. I am the man who was only two days away from being homeless. Yet I stayed on course by God's grace, and now I lead Atlanta's largest church congregation, a flock of twenty-five thousand. Most of my people already know me, but when people first come to New Birth Missionary Baptist Church, they may be tempted to misjudge me when they look at the car I drive and the honor the people give me as their pastor and bishop. But once they find out that the same Bishop Long who now drives a Mercedes used to walk everywhere, that he knows what it is like to lose everything and come to the brink of homelessness, they think, *Oh, he's like us. He knows what it's like.*

When people hear me admit that I was once fired by Ford Motor Company for making personal phone calls, they think, *This man wears the robes of a bishop, but he knows what it's like out in the corporate world. He knows about the pressures I face. In fact, he knows what it is like to give in to that pressure, too.* If I never shared my failures and weaknesses with people, they wouldn't think I had any credibility to talk to them about such things. I understand that when people see a preacher step behind a pulpit, they think, *What does he know?* So I tell them what I know. I tell them how God saved me. I tell them that I am a walking miracle of God who is still in awe that God could and would choose to use me. Then I start on them.

"Do you believe God's Word is true?"

"Yes, sir, every word."

"Do you believe God loves you and has a plan for your life, too?"

"Yes, Bishop. I believe all of that."

"All right. Is your life being overtaken by sin? Are you choosing to do everything but the things God told you to do? Why?"

Most people in the church have a ready excuse: "You don't understand, Bishop. I've got problems."

No, we don't understand God's purpose for the church. We have a bigger problem than our problems! We've got a head commitment to Jesus Christ, but our hearts and bodies haven't caught up yet. It's time to get ourselves in order so we can take our place in God's plan and start living. God has given us everything we need to succeed and live a life for Jesus. No excuse will do when we stand before Him.

## THE LION IS COMING

Perhaps God has sent the spirit of Elijah to modern John the Baptists in our generation to prepare again the way for the coming of the Lord. If that is the case, then we can be sure Jesus Christ won't come as a meek, sacrificial Lamb this time. He finished that mission more than two thousand years ago. This time He will come to take over this planet as the Lion of Judah, not roll to over as the kitten of the kingdom.

> *Jesus is coming to take over this planet as the Lion of Judah.*

He is the King of Kings and Lord of Lords, and it is time for us to acknowledge it. God wants us to be unconventional enough to challenge the status quo in every place and every situation where it opposes the Word and will of God. That means we need to take our stand for truth in both the public marketplace and the church sanctuary.

I knew God was having His way in our church family and in my ministry when we started seeing people by the hundreds relocate to Atlanta from distant cities such as New York

City and Chicago just because they heard that "sound" of God in our ministry. We don't pretend to be the only source of truth or anointing in God's kingdom; there are many more right in the city of Atlanta, as well as throughout North America and the world. But we have learned to take God's call and challenge seriously.

My heart aches for men who leave the major men's meetings each summer after having their hopes lifted up over a weekend, only to go home to near or total spiritual starvation. Although many men who attend events such as the Promise Keepers conventions come from strong, Christ-centered churches who preach the truth from God's Word, some men are trapped in spiritually dead churches where the Holy Spirit is not welcome and God's Word is not preached. I pray that these men's meetings will continue as long as God blesses them, but I also know God said to me, "I want you to get this word out to the hungry. I want you to speak out and write down the things I have given you from My Word so others can receive them and take a bold stand for Me."

Nearly every month of the year, I meet hundreds of men who hear what I say and lift their heads to respond, but they are still stuck in sin or in a church system that honors man and man's traditions more than the living God. I want these men to hear the "different sound" of God's voice and be so challenged that they must step out of the bondage that binds them.

I've often had men tell me the same things after a meeting: "I'm glad to find out that I haven't lost my mind. I never thought I would hear somebody saying the same things that I am hearing God speak to my spirit! It is like a breath of fresh air. I said to myself, 'There has to be somebody bold enough to say what I've been thinking.'"

## SIGNS OF THE TIMES

The church has been hindered for countless years and generations because it has openly dismissed this basic foundational building block of God's purpose. Now God is issuing a summons and a challenge to every church body and leader with ears to hear. He is about to bring judgment to the church, and He is doing it for our own good. The truth is that God is out to help us become true Christians. What we have now isn't working at all, and we are totally unprepared for what is coming.

> If you have run with the footmen, and they have wearied you, then how can you contend with horses? And if in the land of peace, in which you trusted, they wearied you, then how will you do in the floodplain of the Jordan?
> (Jeremiah 12:5)

The horses of change are on the move, and believers around the world are sensing in their spirits that God has stepped up the tempo. He is looking for people who can run with Him. We think we have done well surviving our daily trials and temptations in times of peace, but God wants us to realize that the challenges in front of us are bigger than what is behind. The things we have endured and accomplished so far were only strengthening exercises for where we are going.

145

### YOU ARE THE LIGHT OF THE WORLD

*You are the light of the world. A city that is set on a hill cannot be hidden. Nor do they light a lamp and put it under a basket, but on a lampstand, and it gives light to all who are in the house. Let your light so shine before men, that they may see your good works and glorify your Father in heaven.* (Matthew 5:14–16)

We need to take the basket off and boldly shine the light God gave us. Socrates said, "The life which is unexamined is not worth living." Have you noticed that the church—meaning both her individual members and her public spokesmen—is very skilled and quick to criticize, protest against, and run down everybody? Then maybe you have also noticed that the church doesn't like looking at herself.

People may get angry with me, but I refuse to let this point die. I am compelled by the Spirit of God to say it is a great disgrace and a serious indictment against the church when we point our fingers of religious self-righteousness at the sin we see in the world when our own countless sins of hypocrisy and disobedience to God are heaped high within our own doors. The church is stuck in a rut of her own making. We are trapped in a maze of man-made ordinances, regulations, and authority structures that God never authored or authorized.

The church we have today is not the glorious church of power, light, and holiness pictured in the Bible. Something has to change, and God says it is about to change now. Judgment and mercy begin in the house of God, and then they move outward to the unredeemed world. God is determined to take away the old; then He will bring in the new.

God called us to light His lamp and stand on a hill for the world to see, but we have insisted on having private club meetings instead so we can celebrate our exclusive membership in God's club without interruption from "outsiders."

We cannot ignore the fact that we almost never see an obvious change in our nation when hundreds of thousands of Christians march in Washington, D.C., or gather for other large conventions around the nation. God created everyone as a

> *God called us to light His lamp and stand on a hill for the world to see.*

spiritual being, and people around this nation are desperately looking for a spiritual experience. They want to see some sign that God really exists and that He has the power to change lives for the better.

The world wants to see more than an outward demonstration and show of force. The world wants to see the demonstration of a life changed within by the awesome power of God. If the church continues to fail to offer them the real thing, the people will quickly go after a counterfeit.

## LET US EXAMINE OUR WAYS

We have to stop this mockery of God's purpose for the church. The writer of the book of Lamentations said: *"Let us search out and examine our ways, and turn back to the LORD"* (Lamentations 3:40).

While God is working to mature the people in His church by allowing them to walk through various trials, His

147

less-discerning ministers and pastors are trying to preach the people out of those trials! Therefore, God's people start begging Him for quick fixes to their long-term problems. They just might get what they are asking for. When the children of Israel were in the wilderness, they started complaining about the manna God had given them. They decided that what they needed was meat instead. So God said, "Okay, you want quail? Quail it is."

> *Then you [Moses] shall say to the people, "Consecrate your-selves for tomorrow, and you shall eat meat; for you have wept in the hearing of the LORD, saying, 'Who will give us meat to eat? For it was well with us in Egypt.' Therefore the Lord will give you meat, and you shall eat. You shall eat, not one day, nor two days, nor five days, nor ten days, nor twenty days, but for a whole month, until it comes out of your nostrils and becomes loathsome to you, because you have despised the LORD who is among you, and have wept before Him, saying, 'Why did we ever come up out of Egypt?'"* (Numbers 11:18–20)

God answered the Israelites' prayer for a quick fix, for an early deliverance from God's maturity process, but it cost them dearly. When they complained about the difficulty of their trial and longed for the good old days of slavery under Pharaoh when they had meat to eat, God gave them quail—and He also sent leanness to their souls. (See Psalm 106:13–15.)

He was saying, "You got out too quickly. This was all part of your training. I know when it's time to bring you out of this, and I know what I'm doing. Since you feel you know better, you can reap what you have sown."

I tell the people at New Birth: "If you're going through something difficult, if you feel that you are going through hell, I have one piece of advice for you: Don't stop. Ask God, 'What is it You are trying to teach me? What is it You want to show me through this?'"

The church is not here to bail everybody out of their problems. I am firmly convinced that some of us in the body of Christ are supposed to get our houses repossessed! This may sound radical and even heretical to you, but I have to tell you that everywhere I see great victory, faith, and accomplishments in God's Word, I also see great perseverance in the face of great suffering. It is my conviction that when we preach against the process of maturity in the Christian life, we preach against the order of God.

> *Every great victory comes from great perseverance in suffering.*

God is looking for those disciples who understand that it is impossible to please God without faith. He is trying to help us grow up by marching us into such levels of maturity that we will be able to accomplish His purposes on this earth. It can only be done with the "God kind of faith."

*It takes God to believe God fully.* (See Galatians 2:20.) Don't write this off as a cute religious phrase. When God really speaks to you, I can guarantee that you don't and won't have enough faith on your own to believe Him. You have to have enough God in you to hook up with God speaking to you. The only way you can accomplish the things God is calling you to do is to have so much God in you that you can believe Him supernaturally.

"Now I hope you didn't just make that up, Bishop." No, if you have a problem with this theology, then you need to talk to the Lord about it. My Bible tells me that *"it is God who works in you both to will and to do for His good pleasure"* (Philippians 2:13). The only thing we bring to the table of God is our obedience—even our faith must come from Him. (See Romans 12:3.) Our first and most important "work" in this life is to believe Jesus. Then He gives us everything we need to do the rest of the work He has called us to do.

> *Jesus answered and said to them, "This is the work of God, that you believe in Him whom He sent." Therefore they said to Him, "What sign will You perform then, that we may see it and believe You? What work will You do?"*
>
> (John 6:29–30)

## Stepping Out of the Boat

Whenever God speaks to His Son, the Son moves immediately without conferring with flesh and blood. Now—and watch this—the reason most saints and soldiers never get to the place God ordained for them is that they want to look for evidence *before they move or act.* We ridicule the scribes and Pharisees of Jesus' day, but then we turn around and act just like them. The moment Jesus tells us the work He's called us to do, we ask for a sign.

The second thing we do is react in fear instead of faith. That is a sure sign we haven't died to self so we can live in Christ. We are too afraid of losing our self to live for Him. This robs us of the faith of God residing within us. We say, "God, that's impossible. I can't do that. It's too big for me. I'm afraid. I might get killed. I can't go there. I can't do that."

I'm convinced our problem isn't that we haven't heard God. We've heard God's voice all right; we are just too afraid to do what He has ordained. We are too busy looking for a sign as all of the crowds that followed Jesus did. Then they backed off when the risk of obedience became too great.

> *But the boat was now in the middle of the sea, tossed by the waves, for the wind was contrary. Now in the fourth watch of the night Jesus went to them, walking on the sea. And when the disciples saw Him walking on the sea, they were troubled, saying, "It is a ghost!" And they cried out for fear. But immediately Jesus spoke to them, saying, "Be of good cheer! It is I; do not be afraid." And Peter answered Him and said, "Lord, if it is You, command me to come to You on the water." So He said, "Come." And when Peter had come down out of the boat, he walked on the water to go to Jesus. But when he saw that the wind was boisterous, he was afraid; and beginning to sink he cried out, saying, "Lord, save me!" And immediately Jesus stretched out His hand and caught him, and said to him, "O you of little faith, why did you doubt?" And when they got into the boat, the wind ceased. Then those who were in the boat came and worshiped Him, saying, "Truly You are the Son of God."*
>
> (Matthew 14:24–33)

Our situation is serious. Change has to happen in the church today. God is looking for some crazy Peters who will dare to take risks at His command, even in the middle of a storm. I don't know about you, but I can't remember when I wasn't living in a storm. There has always been a storm of some kind blowing and tossing things around in my life. That doesn't mean God wasn't there or that I am some kind of faithless Christian. My biggest problem was that most of the time, I was acting like the eleven in the boat instead of like crazy Peter, the one who dared to step out of his security when Jesus said, "Come."

I am like you. I always had what I thought were good reasons and excuses to stay in the boat. But God is looking for someone who will stop complaining about the storm long enough to hear and obey His voice. If He says, "Walk on the water," He doesn't want us to ask questions. *He wants us to just start walking!*

> *God is looking for Peters who will take risks even in the storm.*

Now you may be saying, "Bishop, my Bible says Peter started to sink." Yes, my Bible says the same thing. Why? Peter began to sink because he took his eyes off Jesus the Rock and instead looked at the circumstances—the wind and the waves.

### COWERING IN THE "BOAT OF WHAT WAS"

I am convinced that Peter, the professional sailor and fisherman, had already seen those waves. He had measured the intensity of the wind long before he stepped out of the boat. He had already assessed those problems, yet he dismissed them when he heard his Master's voice.

But something helped him turn his eyes away from Jesus and on to those old circumstances again, and I think his problem was that the wind was talking. You see, whenever the wind blows, it can carry voices with it. There were eleven frightened (and probably jealous) men who were still cowering in the boat of man's ingenuity, telling Peter to get back on the "firm" wooden deck of the "boat of what was."

"You can't do that, Peter. How can you know that is really Jesus? After all, that's a spirit out there. You are messing us up. We need your strong back at the oars. Get back on this boat!" There is a good chance that Peter started listening to the crowd for just a moment—and the crowd has never been right as far as God's kingdom goes. God has never led, fed, or said something by majority vote. No, God is still looking for somebody who will step away from everybody else and dare to obey His challenge to change.

The problem with most church folk is that they need a crowd to think they are following God. It is true that crowds gathered where Jesus went, but only disciples followed Christ to the cross and beyond. That's the reason why our churches are only half full for intercessory prayer meetings and work days. The other half is following the crowd. That is why only a handful will show up for the evangelism outreach trip to the wrong side of the tracks; the rest of the "gang of eleven" are clinging to the "home boat" and griping about the few who said yes to change.

We just don't want to go through God's process. We would rather stay in the old system and cling to the old stuff that doesn't work. We don't want to be enlarged because it stretches us beyond our comfort zone. I can promise you this: Whatever God wants you to do right now as an individual and as a member of a local body of believers cannot be accomplished with the narrow and shallow foundation you have today. He has to enlarge and stretch you.

When God places a call or vision in your life, by definition it is supernatural. It cannot ever be accomplished with your strength, resources, or abilities. It will take God to pull it off, so why even play the game of saying, "God, I can't do it"? Of course you can't! Why would God ask you to do something that you could do in your own strength? You wouldn't need His provision, His wisdom, or His power to do it. In other words, it would then be a work of the flesh. Trust me, God doesn't work that way.

> *God doesn't call us to do things in our own strength. Then we wouldn't need Him.*

God wants to pull you out of your boat today because He's about to lay something on the church that is going to revolutionize the world! He is saying, "I need steadfast, immovable, always abounding people. I need people who have been through the fire, people who came through with My Word clenched in their fists. I'm looking for the kind of people who know what it means to break through impossible situations with My Word. They have been stretched with My Word and still managed to hang on, even when it seemed that the thing I promised them wasn't going to happen. I'm looking for a people who will consent to go all the way through the process and emerge with enlarged spirits, vision, and faith."

God is looking for people who have mountain-moving faith! Jesus said, *"Assuredly, I say to you, if you have faith as a mustard seed, you will say to this mountain, 'Move from here to there,' and it will move; and nothing will be impossible for you"* (Matthew 17:20).

Learn to speak to whatever mountain rises up in your presence in opposition to God's revealed will for your life and those in your care. You can command it to get out of the way, but not by your might or power. Speak the word of command by the Spirit.

### THE PROCESS OF GOD

The mustard seed is so small that it is difficult to conceive of its being worthy of mention in a teaching on mountain-moving power. Stranger still, Jesus mentioned the mustard seed as something you can easily plant in the ground. This little seed is so small that it can barely be seen above ground; then it must be buried in the ground out of sight before it can produce anything. You have to put a little dirt on it and compress soil on top of it—in other words, it goes through the process of death and burial.

In a way, this is the same process you and I go through every time we get pregnant with God's promise. Things just seem to get worse before they get better—but nothing is wrong. It is just the process of God.

Now, when that tiny mustard seed is separated from the other mustard seeds and removed from the light of day, from the wind, and from the life-sustaining rain, its only company is darkness and dirt. I thank God that He designed seeds not to operate by sight. In a sense, the darkness and dirt are telling the seed, "You aren't getting out—you are just a tiny seed caught in our grip far from the light. You are dead."

Even as you read these words, you may feel as if you have already been eulogized by the darkness, and the dirt has been piled on top of you. You have heard it all: "This is your lot in life. You are stuck in this place! You'll never taste joy again. You will never have pleasure in your life. You are old. You are sick and weak. You're condemned to die where you lie."

Take courage from the tiny mustard seed that says: I am not a seed. I may look like a seed, but I'm really a giant tree. In God's perfect time I am going to be a tree. After a while I'm coming up out of this darkness and exploding from the dirt into the light. Then I will be the master over the dirt, and I will draw strength from the very thing that tried to bury me. So you can talk about me

> *Though the mustard seed is tiny, it says, "I'm a tree!"*

today, you can pick on me for a season, but I believe what God says about me. No matter what you say or do, I'm going to keep saying, "I'm a tree. I'm a tree. I'm a tree!"

How does that old saying go? "Every mighty oak tree began as a nut that just kept going." If God says your marriage will be resurrected, then don't be surprised if that promise gets buried by mountains of dirt and darkness. Your job is to keep talking about resurrection.

If God tells you He has destroyed the yoke of poverty over your life, then keep speaking the promise of prosperity, even though you may sit in the darkness of lack under a mountain of bills for a season. See the fruit of God's favor before it appears. "I'm going to buy that, and I'm going to finance that for the kingdom. I'm going to lend money, not borrow it."

When God tells you that your church is going to take the city, then start speaking God's truth even when your enemies start lining up to "set you straight," and they will—trust me. I've been there.

Do you know what happens millions of times a year in the Christian world of seminars, conferences, and holy convocations? Every time believers go to an anointed conference (the other kind don't count), they go home feeling wonderful, delivered, renewed, and redeemed for the first three weeks. But by the fourth or fifth week they are feeling bad again, and they find themselves sliding back into same old routine they had hoped to break by attending the conference!

## "Just Grease Me Down"

I used to go to every conference I could find, and I went up for prayer every time I could. I should have just told those ministers, "Just grease me down with that anointing oil." I'd go to the South for a conference one week and rush to the North for another conference the next week. I did everything I could to get an instant fix to my problems without the pain of self-discipline.

I didn't want to study. I didn't want to labor. If I located an anointed man of God, I would automatically ask him lay his hands on me. I even got upset if a preacher would bypass me to lay hands on someone else. Usually I would end up chasing him down the prayer line just so I could stick my head under his hands as he prayed. It became a compulsion.

### PREGNANT WITH PROMISE

Some of us do not want to go through the process of maturing, but it is God's divine process for birthing holy things in us, in the church, and in the world. No matter how much we want them, there are no shortcuts to God's process. He is looking for people who don't need a whole lot of evidence to move. Every time you hear God's voice and obey, your confidence is built in His Word.

Mothers who have already given birth to a child are much calmer and steadier than first-time mothers. It is the same with seasoned disciples.

> **When you hear God's voice and obey, your confidence is built.**

They aren't worried about the process of stretching, and they don't mind the discomfort and unsettled feeling of pregnancy. They know what comes at the end of God's process—new life, new joy, a new measure of power and glory, and a new horizon of opportunity in Christ.

My wife tells me that once she started dilating when she was having our baby, she wondered if she was going to make it. Many women start screaming at their doctors, "Give me something! Get this kid out now! I quit! I don't want to do this."

Once you start having the contractions in your Holy Ghost pregnancy, you may think they are from the devil! The problem is that you will suddenly be tempted to kick that word of promise out before its time. When you're having contractions, you need to know that they are from God so you can see them through to the end and possess what God has ordained for you.

STRETCH MARKS

It is easy to get irritated with the growing trend among young married ladies these days who say, "Oh, I don't want to get pregnant too soon. I don't want to have any babies because I don't want to mess up my figure." This is especially hard to swallow for women who have been through some labor and deliveries. They have paid the price to give birth to new life; they have received some stretch marks in the process.

Sometimes God will stretch you when He gives you a word of promise. The holy thing you bring to term will leave some permanent marks on you, but it isn't anything to be ashamed of. Those are witnessing points.

Someone may say, "Oh, you haven't been through anything. How would you know how I feel?" Then all you have to do is open up your coat and say, "Let me show you my stretch marks. Let me tell you what will work for you. I know it will work, because it worked for me. I know what it is like to wait and wait, and then wait some more. I know what it is like to pray and fast until I thought I couldn't do it anymore—but here I am. I made it. Here are pictures of my children."

That is the same thing that Jesus did when He confronted doubting Thomas. He said, *"Reach your finger here, and look at My hands; and reach your hand here, and put it into My side. Do not be unbelieving, but believing"* (John 20:27).

159

When I first heard the call of the Lord to preach, I obeyed because I knew I had heard His voice. I was doing well at the time—I basically took a cut in pay of thirty thousand dollars to start at my church. But later on—I said later on—God gave it all back to me and more.

Yet even in the place of obedience, I was in the midst of a storm because God wanted me to change. I woke up one day and said, "This thing has to be real, or I am getting out." Well, I discovered that God is real, and so is His power. I also discovered that there is a price attached to the real thing. Salvation is a free gift, but discipleship costs you everything. There is a cross with my name on it overshadowing my "Disciple of Jesus" badge. The badge is easy to put on, but the cross will kill you. That has been God's plan all along—kill the old man and raise up the new.

> *Salvation is a free gift, but discipleship costs you everything.*

I told my congregation during a celebration of God's Year of Jubilee that the Lord was saying, "During this Year of Jubilee, your labor is going to begin. It is going to be so rough that you will have to forgive some people and get rid of all of your hidden bitterness. You see, the baby God planted in your womb is going to force every deep-rooted thing out of you."

## LABOR PAINS AND GENUINE CHANGE

During your labor to deliver God's seed in your life, He will cause the labor pains to hit you extra hard in areas where you need deliverance. Yes, you will have that baby in due time, but right now you are in the middle of something else. You might be saying, "Lord, I don't feel like myself. I just don't feel right."

God doesn't want you to feel like yourself—Christ is being formed in you. Something new and holy is being developed in you, and you won't get through the process without being stretched, expanded, and pressed beyond your normal measure. You're not going to get through this without some stretch marks, but don't stop the process! There is a great reward in the end.

God is looking for individuals and churches who are mature enough to go through a second birth. He is looking for a people who will submit to the stretching, discomfort, and labor required for Christ to be formed in them as a witness to the world. If you say, "Be it done to me according to Your will" (see Luke 1:38), then He will cause you to change as never before. He will speak things into you that sound crazy and absolutely impossible, but don't be alarmed.

He is setting you up for victory on a whole new level, but what He is about to do won't follow any man-pleasing pattern. You won't get there following any preset recipe, formula, or agenda of man. The way of the seed coming from darkness and pressure below to light and glory above is the path of persistent obedience to God and unyielding faith in His promises. When He speaks, you must be obedient and faithful enough to change without question. For nine months you will stretch, expand, and experience all of the discomforts of change. But then the day will come for your final labor that leads to a miraculous delivery.

## No Compromise

God has set His course, and His Word is destined to penetrate and cut through every spiritual barrier that we have built to protect ourselves. The Lord knows that our paradigms and man-made traditions will keep us from moving in the dimension He has ordained. He is out to take over, and He is in no mood to compromise or coddle.

I am convinced that millions of Christians around the world are hearing God say the same things I have heard.

I urge you by the Spirit of God to lay aside every weight that has so easily entangled you in the past. Make a clean break from the past today. Press forward for the mark of your high calling in Christ Jesus. March on, lifting high the torch of God's truth. It is time to rise and answer God's call to a higher standard. It is time to leave compromise and concerns about past failures behind. It is time to take back what the devil has stolen!

CHAPTER 6

# A Mandate for the Individual

As we marched through Atlanta in December 2004, I had a transcendent sense that we were prophets, joined together as one person to declare the dominion of God to principalities and powers, as well as to the nation and the world. Yet, we were *individuals* united, each maintaining and declaring our own part in God's great procession.

God is marching through the earth, and you have a place in that divinely orchestrated parade—a unique and divinely crafted position that none but you can fill. Mature saints are coming together in one last great union to manifest the spiritual body of Jesus Christ before His return.

We were all walking as one. Everyone was just satisfied to be where they should be—not pushing to go somewhere else. The greatest peace that you can experience is to know, "This is why I was born." No one can beat you at being what God ordained you to be. Resting in that place of completion will free you from the pressure of wanting to be someone else.

As you assume your individual rank and file in the procession of God, you will find it impossible to hate anyone else. You'll be satisfied and comforted to know no one can beat me being the toe in the body of Christ; everything comes under subjection to the feet and we walk in dominion. (See 1 Corinthians 12:27.) As we mature in Christ, we find dominion through fully expressing our individuality of giftedness in union with the rest of Christ's body of believers. *"Now you are the body of Christ, and members individually"* (1 Corinthians 12:27). That means that you as an individual are to take dominion as you connect with others in the body.

> ## "Why was I born?" You are here to take dominion.

Your dominion is your destiny in Christ. Therefore, it is vitally important that you rise up to your full, mature purpose in the earth, which involves becoming a fully functioning position in the march.

### YOUR DOMINION IS YOUR DESTINY

Did you ever ask: "Why was I born? Why did God place me in the earth?" You are here to take dominion. That exalted purpose for being was first established in the Genesis 1:26:

> *Then God said, "Let Us make man in Our image, according to Our likeness; let them have dominion over the fish of the sea, over the birds of the air, and over the cattle, over all the earth and every creeping thing that creeps on the earth."*

Even after the fall, God never changed His mind from the stated purpose: *"Let them have dominion."* Mankind did

164

not lose the promise of dominion, and God did not renege on His purpose for us. In fact, Christ came to restore our position back to God so that we could resume our purpose, place, and position in the earth. Romans 8:19 speaks of this promise of full restoration when it says, *"For the earnest expectation of the creation eagerly waits for the revealing of the sons of God."*

There is a lot of talk about the body of Christ and the kingdom of God operating in the earth. But in reality, most members of the body of Christ are living like atheists when it comes to this truth. We preach a present-day reality of the kingdom, but we act as if it doesn't really exist. There's no use in being a king if you are not in charge of anything. For Revelation 5:10 says, *"And have made us kings and priests to our God; and we shall reign on the earth."* (See also 1 Peter 2:9.)

Taking charge means walking in dominion, a lost position of spiritual authority and privilege that needs to be taken back. Let's take a closer look at this foundational passage in Genesis that establishes our right and responsibility of dominion...

### Dominion Over Fish

Dominion in Genesis 1:26 begins with our position over the seas, for it says, *"Let them have dominion over the fish of the sea."* This concerns the natural realm, but it doesn't stop there. The principle of spiritual interpretation established in 1 Corinthians 15 suggests that a principle is first established in the natural, and then in the spiritual. *"However, the spiritual is not first, but the natural, and afterward the spiritual"* (1 Corinthians 15:46).

In other words, mankind was given dominion over the fish of the sea, the natural fish. But a second spiritual reading is possible, also. Throughout Scripture, God refers to mankind as fish of the sea. The disciples were told to become fishers of men, in one instance, and there are many more. In another parable, the kingdom of God is likened to fishermen who have caught a great haul. These fish are clearly considered the living souls of men and women.

The prophet Jonah's story focused upon a great fish. He was called to minister in Ninevah, but he didn't want to go, so he headed directly in the opposite direction toward Tarshish. When a storm of devastating proportions whipped up and threatened the boat, the sailors learned of Jonah's disobedience and threw him into the water. But God had prepared a fish to swallow him. The Bible tells us he went to the very gates of hell.

> *As soon as you call, God will bring you back to dry land.*

Jonah's troubles started with his own disobedience, but ended up in triumph. Still, between the tragedy and triumph was an extended trip into hell. Jonah, according to the Word, was in the belly of the fish for three days, and it also indicates that during this time he visited hell.

Your journey is no different. Many of the tragedies in your life are of your own making, and your triumphs will be the gift of God to you. In between, you will go through a death and resurrection that will take you to your destined purpose. We all must follow Christ and take up our crosses of suffering and death, in order to gain resurrection power in our lives and ministries. Some of the things you are going through are intended to get you focused so you can learn to pray. God will prepare a problem and show you what hell looks like, and as soon as you call Him, He'll bring you back to dry land.

Every saint destined to power and authority will experience some measure of His death, burial, and resurrection. I don't care how low you go, how bad it gets, or how far down into your valley you must walk. You will experience death there, but you will also find resurrection. You will learn to acknowledge, "When God gets ready to bring me up, He will. I will be put out on dry land."

Jonah got thrown off the boat in the middle of the ocean by those surrounding him. In your life, they may call you a troublemaker, but God has something prepared for you. Let them eulogize you and talk about you, because what you think is a curse is really a blessing. A day will come when He's ready to release you, and you'll say, "I'm coming up, and I'm coming

> *Every valley in your life is ready to be exalted.*

higher than I was before. I don't care how low I've been; God said I'm coming up. The devil is not going to steal my joy. I'm not going to let my current situation steal my joy, because my financial situation is ready to be resurrected."

I sense that you are coming out of the valley right now. Every valley in your life is getting ready to be exalted. (See Isaiah 40:4.) You may feel dead, but life is being breathed back into you. Your friends and family may have buried you, but you're getting ready to come right out of the grave like Lazarus.

No matter how deep your depression or debt or sexual addiction, God says, "I've given you dominion, and you're ready to get back up."

Jesus went to hell to get the keys to death, hell, and the grave. Your trip to hell was to gain authority in your situation. Your experience in hell made some changes to you that had to be made. God put you through some things so you'd become sick and tired of your sin. Now, instead of defeat, you'll be able to say, "I have authority in that area of my life." Because of your trip to hell, what once held you can't hold you any longer. What kept you bound, can bind you no longer.

There will be physical manifestations because you're getting up, you're coming back from your hell. You went to hell to take back your dignity; you went to hell to take back your self-respect; you went to hell to take back your self-control. You're coming back, but you'll never again be the same. The favor of God has been placed upon your life.

## Dominion Over the Birds of the Air

God didn't give mankind dominion over the fish and nothing else. He also gave them dominion over the birds of the air. These represent principalities and powers, demonic forces, and the prince of the power of the air. Most saints don't take dominion over the birds of the air.

In Genesis 15, Abraham was entering into covenant with God and preparing the sacrifice. The Scripture says that birds started flying down at the sacrifice, trying to eat it up. Abraham had to stand over that sacrifice and shoo away the birds:

[God] *said to him* [Abram], *"Bring Me a three-year-old heifer, a three-year-old female goat, a three-year-old ram, a turtledove, and a young pigeon." Then he brought all these to Him and cut them in two, down the middle, and placed each piece opposite the other; but he did not cut the birds in two. And when the vultures came down on the carcasses, Abram drove them away.* (Genesis 15:9–11)

Anytime you try to get closer to God and walk in His ways, the devil will try to hinder you. You'll get home and find bad news in the mail or your spouse will be angry with you.

Jesus said, *"Behold, a sower went out to sow. And as he sowed, some seed fell by the wayside; and the birds came and devoured them"* (Matthew 13:3–4). As soon as the sower sowed the word, the birds came to steal what was sown. Birds are the spirits that fly in the outer places where the Word has been sown, trying to devour the seed before it grows.

You hear God's Word, and you receive faith in your heart to conquer your poverty or your addiction. But before you leave the church, thoughts come flying through your head, saying, "No one can fix the debt I'm in. Not even God." "I'll die in my addiction." Or, "I might as well get a divorce. No one can save my marriage." These are spirits trying to fly into your covenant with God to rob you by filling you with doubt.

Sunday by Sunday, by the time you get to your car go to go home, thoughts are filling your head with doubt, robbing you of what the Lord has planted into your life. Just as Abraham shooed away those vultures, you must learn to take authority over those thoughts that try to exalt themselves against the Word of God.

For some of us, our greatest problem is allowing thoughts contrary to God's will to fill our minds and hearts. Eventually these form strongholds. Second Corinthians 10:4 says, *"For the weapons of our warfare are not carnal but mighty in God for pulling down strongholds."*

Did God breathe into you today, saying, "This is your great getting up morning"? Don't let doubt fill your mind. Faith works beyond the realm of facts and reason. God often violates our "facts," because He is truth.

> ## Let God breathe into you, saying, "This is your morning."

He says that all things are possible to him who believes. (See Matthew 17:20.) Therefore, shoo away every thought, every bird sent to rob your faith and steal your promises.

### EVICT THE DEVIL

If you've ever owned rental property, you may understand how difficult evicting a tenant can be. Yet there are certain times when it must be done. There are some thoughts, some birds, that have nested in your mind for years, and they are killing your joy and your spirit. Everyone around you has been affected by them. Take dominion over those birds and evict them right now in the name of Jesus.

Some of us really don't want to get rid of some of the birds that rob us. When the beggar got healed at the temple gate, he really didn't ask to be healed. He wanted money. Getting healed meant a total and uncomfortable change in his life-style. Healing would require getting a job and leaving all the other beggar friends he'd known.

Some of us have lived such pitiful lives for so long that we don't know if we want to be well. Getting delivered will mean learning to take responsibility. It will mean leaving all we've known, and that can feel very scary.

When Jonah came out of the fish, he was spit on dry ground. For you, every place the sole of your foot shall tread is given to you. (See Joshua 1:3.) Where you are standing is yours already, so take dominion over it. Perhaps you think your journey into hell caused you to lose time in God's plan and purpose for your life. You haven't lost a moment. God's clock had your valley factored in, and although it seemed like a side trail, you've been moving directly forward. And now that you're leaving your valley, God says, "I'm going to shoot you into the right position and then give you a promotion."

# CHAPTER 7

# THE MARCH OF THE REDEEMED

There lies ahead a great, holy march of God's children coming to meet Him in triumphal procession. Every tribe, kindred, tongue, and family will be represented together with those from ages past. Some will dance and sing the songs of Asia. Some will rejoice and shout in English. Some will worship in the tongues of Africa, all while Europeans—Russians, Swedes, French, and Germans—present themselves before His magnificent throne.

It will be a time of resurrection power like no other. But when that glorious day finally comes, will you be ready?

## A GREATER FAITH

Those standing before the Lord on that great day will be clothed in white garments, which symbolize resurrection power. The saints on that day will walk and live in the power of resurrection, but to get there they'll have to experience death. They will have journeyed through the valley and been covered under its shadow. The march through that valley must precede the triumphant procession, which means you have a position in both parades.

To understand this principle a little better, let's look at the story of Lazarus:

> *Now a certain man was sick, Lazarus of Bethany, the town of Mary and her sister Martha. It was that Mary who anointed the Lord with fragrant oil and wiped His feet with her hair, whose brother Lazarus was sick. Therefore the sisters sent to Him, saying, "Lord, behold, he whom You love is sick."* (John 11:1–3)

When Jesus heard that Lazarus was dying, instead of coming right away, he waited two more days until his close friend died. Mary and Martha were deeply disappointed knowing Jesus had the power to heal Lazarus while he was sick, but He didn't come right away.

You may be in similar circumstances right now. You've prayed for Jesus to come and fix your problem, deliver you, or set you free from affliction or pain. But Jesus seems to be delayed, and your circumstances have gotten increasingly worse. You may be more confused right now than Mary and Martha were when their brother died.

*God wants to stretch your faith to believe for greater things.*

Mary and Martha believed Jesus could heal Lazarus if he were alive but sick, but they lacked faith to believe Jesus could bring their brother back to life after he died. Maybe God wants to stretch your faith to believe for greater things than you understand.

In verse 14 Jesus plainly told His disciples: *"Lazarus is dead."* And in verses 21–22, Martha revealed great faith: *"Then*

*Martha said to Jesus, 'Lord, if You had been here, my brother would not have died. But even now I know that whatever You ask of God, God will give You.'"*

Maybe you are in deadly circumstances and feel that God hasn't shown up. Somehow you've continued to sense His presence, so you are confused. You're saying, "I know it appears to be hopeless, but God…I know if You want to do it, You can."

## You Will Rise Again

Jesus responded to Martha, *"Your brother will rise again"* (John 11:23).

Have you fallen when you were trying to follow God's will? We talk about folk who fall when they are tempted to do bad things, but what about falling when you're doing what is right? Perhaps you worked hard at a job and still got fired because you became a scapegoat for someone else's failure. Or, maybe your marriage has failed, even though you worked hard to be a good wife or husband. Somehow it just exploded in front of you, and you're left with a giant hole in your heart and you can't figure out where God went.

You're disappointed with God. If only He had been there, your spouse wouldn't have taken up with the other person, the baby wouldn't gotten sick and died, or you'd still have your job. I have an announcement for you: Jesus is saying, "You shall rise again."

*Jesus said to her, "I am the resurrection and the life. He who believes in Me, though he may die, he shall live. And whoever lives and believes in Me shall never die. Do you believe this?"* (John 11:25–26)

Jesus made His way to the tomb, but a great big boulder was covering the mouth of the cave. Jesus commanded, *"Take away the stone"* (verse 39).

## ROLL AWAY THE STONE

Perhaps the reason you feel so despondent is that a great big boulder lies between you and your blessing. You need someone to move the stone. What I mean is that you need a little help regarding the miracle you're seeking. Maybe you need a little strength or some resources you just don't have right now. There have been some seasons I felt so low that somebody had to reach down and help me up. I didn't just wake up one morning and get up—somebody had to call me. I needed the hand of someone else to reach into my despair and darkness and yank me out.

*Jesus said, "Take away the stone." Martha, the sister of him who was dead, said to Him, "Lord, by this time there is a stench, for he has been dead four days."* (John 11:39)

When Jesus ordered the stone be moved, Martha protested that after four days dead, the body would stink. Have you ever assisting rolling back the stone of another's dilemma only to warn the Lord that the person stinks? Some people have been in sin for so long that they continue to reek long after they are saved. But God doesn't need you to warn Him about the stench of another person.

If God tells you to help someone out, then help. Be obedient to the Lord without protest. He doesn't need you to tell

Him that person stinks, because, in truth, if you weren't wearing cologne you might not smell so good yourself. It's amazing how we discern everybody else's sin, but seldom smell the foul odor of our own.

Lazarus had been dead for four days, and Jesus spoke to Martha about faith. He said, *"Did I not say to you that if you would believe you would see the glory of God?"* (John 11: 40). Afterward, the stone was rolled away. Jesus prayed, and then cried out to Lazarus in a loud voice, *"Lazarus, come forth"* (verse 43). And he who had been dead for four days in the grave came forth alive.

### LAZARUS, COME FORTH!

You, too, are a Lazarus if you've been getting up in the middle of the night because God is calling you to prayer. You are a Lazarus if you've been hearing a sound coming from the Spirit, a call upon your inner man to rise up from where you are in the grave of complacency and inaction. You can't walk yet, but you can begin to believe. There are folks just beyond your field of vision ready and waiting to take off your graveclothes. Everything that has been locked up inside of you is ready to be released.

In the name of Jesus, I'm calling you forth to come out of your tomb! Perhaps you've been dead for a long time; nonetheless, God is ready to bring you out. It would be a shame to die never having truly lived. Jesus said, "I've come that you might have life." (See John 10:10.) Tell the Lord, "Don't count me out."

Maybe everything about your life has pronounced death over you. No one ever expected you to come back from where you've been. You've been in the grave too long. Well, right now, in the name of Jesus Christ, I call you to come forth from your grave. The voice of God is calling to you: *Come forth!*

Jesus never raised a person from the dead in order to prove His power. Martha knew His power. She said, "I know whatever you ask Him, He is going to do." (See John 11:22.) Those around Jesus well understood His power. Yet, He only raised a few people from the dead: among them were Jarius's daughter and Lazarus. He raised these folks from the dead because their destiny was incomplete. God wasn't finished with them; the conclusion of their story had not been written.

> *The voice of God is calling to you: "Come forth!"*

Does that sound like you, too? Are you saying, "God's not through with me yet. I can't go out like this, because He has made promises to me that remain unfulfilled. My story hasn't been completed. It might look to everyone around me as if my life is over, but I'm about to get up again. They're about to witness another resurrection from the dead!"

Maybe you went through a divorce, or maybe you've been battling cancer. Perhaps you've fallen right on your face, financially or morally. Or maybe your dream died a long time ago—so long ago that you haven't spoken about it for years. Those around you have wrapped you up with doubt and negativity as your grave clothes. You've been shrouded so tightly you couldn't move. You've been bound by their unbelief and negative words. They've mourned your death.

If that sounds like you, it's time to rise up and declare: "I'm not finished yet! Eye has not seen, nor has ear heard what God has prepared for me. I'm not dead!"

### LIVING IN A COMA

You even may think you're doing pretty well right now. But, in truth, you've been sleeping walking. Your spirit man has been barely existing, living in a coma. Just because a person is in a coma doesn't mean he or she cannot respond. I went to the hospital recently with another minister to see a young lady who had been in an accident. The nurse kept calling and shaking her. The nurse said, "Just keep calling her name."

"Lazarus, come forth!"

Over the past year, you've experienced a restlessness inside of you. You thought the devil was after you when everything started going wrong. But it's not the devil who has been after you, it was God. God has been calling you, trying to shake you awake, to stir you to come forth from your coma.

"Lazarus, come forth!"

My mama had a way of bringing me to my senses as a child by simply calling my name. She'd say, "Eddie…"

I'd reply, "But, Mama…I…"

"Eddie!"

Something happens when God calls your name. You receive a sense of your destiny, a greater understanding of who you are. You're not all those critical names others have called you. When God calls your name, He launches you into your destiny.

179

## SPEAK INTO THE TOMB

Jesus called loudly right into the tomb where Lazarus lay dead. "Lazarus, come forth!"

Where did you die? Where was it you laid down your vision? When did you give up hope? What day was it when you stopped believing that God could do what He promised? Where were you when you chose to let bitterness consume your heart? What happened when you let someone bury you with doubt, shame, and disappointment?

Show me where you got derailed. Show me who lied to you. Point to the place where your dreams were broken and you stopped dreaming. What made you afraid to dream for fear of disappointment?

> *God never left you and He never let you down. He's always been there.*

Show me where you decided that God would not show you something miraculous in your life; show me where you lost your innocence. Where is the place you believed God let you down? Where were you when your heart said, "Lord, if You had been there..."?

Know this, God never left you and He never let you down. David said,

> *Where can I go from Your Spirit? Or where can I flee from Your presence? If I ascend into heaven, You are there; if I make my bed in hell, behold, You are there. If I take the wings of the morning, and dwell in the uttermost parts of the sea, even there Your hand shall lead me, and Your right hand shall hold me.* (Psalm 139:7–10)

He's always been there. You may have had a pretty tough ride, but the only reason it wasn't rougher still was because of His kindness and care toward you. And the only reason you made it out on the other end was because He held you in the palm of His hand every step of the way. Instead of blaming God, you should be thanking Him for keeping you.

You haven't even lived yet, but you're about to come alive. Do you hear the voice of the Master calling:

"Lazarus, come forth!"

## BREAK THE SEAL

When they buried Lazarus, people sealed him in. In my own life, I have been through some pretty tough stuff, but what made it most difficult to come back were those around me who sealed my fate. What good is it to be forgiven and given a second chance when everyone around you only remembers the stench of death that was on you? Those who seal you in a tomb continue to talk about the old you. Their biting words doom you to forever live under a dark cloud of past mistakes.

Those standing at Lazarus' tomb may have supposed that Jesus would not have the stone unsealed and moved away, but He did. You've been disappointed and discouraged, but did you ever consider why the devil has worked so hard to keep you from your purpose and calling? What does he know about you that you don't even know about yourself? You have needed some help rolling away the stone so you could come out. There's been a lot holding you back. But don't look back over the hindrances, or they will impede your forward progress.

181

Come forth, in the name of Jesus. Everything that limits and hinders you, I curse it and move it out of your way in Jesus' name. Right now, in the name of Jesus, I release you from every demonic force and mental barrier that has held and sealed your destiny. They are destroyed and I declare the peace of God will fill your mind. In the name of Jesus, I curse every spirit that has held you, and I cast these spirits out of you. You are free, for whom the Lord sets free *is* free indeed.

"Lazarus, come forth!"

God did not save you to hold you down. You are alive now, and you can live in prosperity—body, soul, and spirit. You have been delivered, and by His stripes you are healed. Whatever was holding you back can't hold you anymore.

## His Kingdom Come

God is not only calling you to come out of the tomb of spiritual slumber, bondage, and death. He is calling His church as one people to come forth from the grave. *"He has made everything beautiful in its time. Also He has put eternity in their hearts"* (Ecclesiastes 3:11). No one is disqualified from the purposes of God.

> **God is calling His church as one people to come forth from the grave.**

The deliverance of Lazarus was so spectacular that he did not have to give out tracks to convince people to believe. When Lazarus came back home and sat down for a meal with Jesus, everyone came to see him because they heard that the one who had been dead was now alive. Lazarus became a living witness.

The purpose of some of your valleys may have been to make you a witness. When folks see you delivered and hear your story, they will rejoice in the power of God. Thank God for the testimony He has given you. God got the attention of those who had counted you out of the race completely. No matter where you've been or how far down you've fallen, God is well able to pull you out and make you stand.

Before it's all over they'll be praising God along with you, saying: "I am no longer bound. I'm free."

Why not commit your life to His purposes, position, and power afresh right now. This is His mighty mandate in the earth. Our eyes will behold the wonder and our hearts will thrill with the glory of the Lord. What was dead has come alive, and He has made all things new.

It won't be long when we will all rise up in resurrection power to join together in that one great celebration. You will have your part and so will I. We'll stand together before His glorious throne, a throng without number: the march of the redeemed.

## The March of the Redeemed

It will be a march like no other, when all God's children appear before Him in one accord having taken back all that was stolen, bound together in perfection of unity and solidarity of love. We'll throw off our grave clothes for linen robes of light, and we'll exchange garments of mourning for laughter and celebration of our new life in Christ. (See Isaiah 61:3.)

183

It's a march that's been awaited throughout the ages of time and spoken of throughout the pages of Holy Scripture. (See Psalm 68:24.) We'll have our place on that glorious day, singing songs of worship before the glorious throne when the saints of God come marching home.

> *After these things I looked, and behold, a great multitude which no one could number, of all nations, tribes, peoples, and tongues, standing before the throne and before the Lamb, clothed with white robes, with palm branches in their hands, and crying out with a loud voice, saying, "Salvation belongs to our God who sits on the throne, and to the Lamb!"*
>
> (Revelation 7:9–10)

# ABOUT THE AUTHOR

E ddie L. Long is the visionary and leader for New Birth Missionary Baptist Church. Since his installation in 1987, New Birth's membership has quickly multiplied from three hundred to well over twenty-five thousand. In that time, Bishop Long directed numerous building expansions, land acquisitions, and building development efforts. These efforts led to the construction of a thirty-seven-hundred-seat sanctuary in 1991, a Family Life Center in 1999, and a ten-thousand-seat complex in 2001.

Located in the heart of DeKalb County, Georgia, in the city of Lithonia, New Birth Missionary Baptist Church continues to impact the community through countless outreach programs and community-empowering projects. He also serves as the founder and CEO of Faith Academy, New Birth's school of excellence.

A native of North Carolina, Long received his bachelor's degree in business administration from North Carolina Central University and a master's of divinity degree from Atlanta's Interdenominational Theological Center. Additionally, Long has received honorary doctorates from North Carolina Central University, Beulah Heights Bible College of Atlanta, and the Morehouse School of Religion. In 2006, Bishop Long received a pastoral degree in Pastoral Ministry from the International College of Excellence, an affiliate of Life Christian University in Tampa, Florida.

Bishop Long is revered locally, nationally, and internationally as a dynamic man of vision, leadership, integrity and compassion. He serves on an array of boards including: the Morehouse School of Religion Board of Directors, the Board of Visitors for Emory University, the Board of Trustees for North Carolina Central University, the Board of Trustees for Young Life, the Board of Trustees for Fort Valley State University, the Board of Directors for Safehouse Outreach Ministries, and the Board of Trustees for Beulah Heights Bible College. He is also an honorary member of the 100 Black Men of America. Bishop Long has been named one of America's 125 most influential leaders and has received a plethora of awards in recognition to his world changing ministry. A constant advocate for change and awareness, Bishop Long was honored by the Center for Disease Control and the National HIV/AIDS Partnership (NHAP) for his outstanding work in fighting the spread of HIV/AIDS.

In 2004, Bishop Long established a mentorship program known as the Longfellows Summer Academy to assist in the mental, physical, and spiritual development of young men between the ages twelve and sixteen. What began as an eight-week program quickly developed into a life-long commitment. And with this new commitment, Bishop Long began to raise funds earmarked for educational scholarships for the sixty-three charter members of the Longfellow Summer Academy.

Bishop Long's *Taking Authority* broadcast, which is seen in one hundred seventy countries worldwide, has received more than 40 nationally recognized honors. A noted author, Bishop

Long's captivating and powerful messages are masterfully captured in a number of audio and video series including: *I Don't Want Delilah, I Need You; The Spirit of Negativity and Familiarity and Kingdom Relationship; Power of a Wise Woman; What a Man Wants, What a Woman Needs; Called to Conquer; Gladiator: The Strength of a Man; Taking Over,* and his most recent, *It's Your Time.*

In 2006, Bishop Long was honored by the King family to officiate the homegoing ceremonies for Mrs. Coretta Scott King—wife of the late Martin Luther King, Jr.

Bishop Long and his wife, Vanessa, are the proud parents of four children: Eric, Edward, Jared, and Taylor. The couple has also served as surrogate parents for many other children in the church and community.

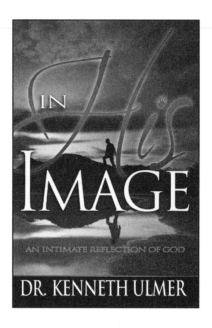

### In His Image:
### An Intimate Reflection of God
*Dr. Kenneth Ulmer*

From a unique perspective, Dr. Kenneth Ulmer explores man's anatomy in an intriguing way—as a physical reflection of God! Throughout Scripture, we learn that God's eyes search, His voice thunders, His hand gives and protects. Discover how God offers you His caring arm during unsteady times when you feel you're at your worst, how He inclines His ear toward you when you need Him to hear your heart, and how His smile radiates when you make choices that reflect His image. This intimate portrait of Him will draw you into a closer understanding of the great love God has for us, His greatest creation.

ISBN: 978-0-88368-993-6 • Hardcover • 208 pages

www.whitakerhouse.com

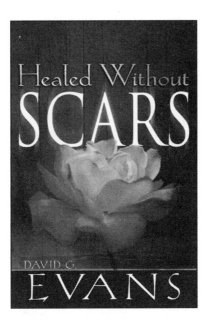

## Healed Without Scars
*David G. Evans*

Have you been hurt by past disappointment, fear, rejection, abandonment, or failure? If so, you've probably learned that time doesn't necessarily heal all wounds. When pain from the past lingers in our lives and causes emotional scars, you need to understand that God is always ready to help you! Discover the path to personal wholeness, and find peace in the midst of life's storms. Renew your hopes and dreams, and experience a life of freedom and joy. For years, author David Evans has helped people from all walks of life learn how to live in victory. Let him guide you to a joyful life of wholeness in Christ as you learn that you can be *Healed Without Scars*!

ISBN: 978-0-88368-542-2 • Trade • 272 pages

WHITAKER
HOUSE
www.whitakerhouse.com

### Free at Last:
### Removing the Past from Your Future
### (with Study Guide CD)
*Larry Huch*

You can break free from your past! Don't let what has happened to you and your family hold you back in life. You can find freedom from depression, anger, abuse, insecurity, and addiction in Jesus Christ. Pastor Larry Huch reveals powerful truths from Scripture that enabled him and many others to quickly break the destructive chains in their lives and receive God's blessings. Learn the secret to true freedom and you, too, can regain your joy and hope, experience divine health, mend broken relationships, walk in true prosperity—body, soul, and spirit.

ISBN: 978-0-88368-428-3 • Trade with CD • 272 pages

---

www.whitakerhouse.com

### More of Him:
### Receiving the Power of the Holy Spirit
### (with CD)
*George G. Bloomer*

Are you walking in power as Christ did? Is your desire for intimacy with the Father increasing? Are you passionately pursuing the Holy Spirit's presence? Prepare to discover a deeper understanding of the indwelling of the Spirit. Don't be lost in this doctrinal tug-of-war. Join Bishop George G. Bloomer as he provides solid, scriptural answers on the Holy Spirit—His person, His fruits, His gifts, His unifying work. There's no need to live in confusion any longer. As you begin to walk in this deeper understanding, you will be filled with new wisdom, power, and strength. Prepare to find *More of Him* and receive the power of the Holy Spirit.

ISBN: 978-0-88368-790-6 • Hardcover w/ CD • 224 pages

WHITAKER
HOUSE

www.whitakerhouse.com

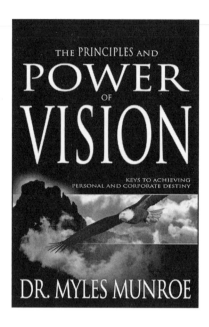

## The Principles and Power of Vision
*Dr. Myles Munroe*

Whether you are a businessperson, a homemaker, a student, or a head of state, best-selling author Dr. Myles Munroe explains how you can make your dreams and hopes a living reality. Your success is not dependent on the state of the economy or what the job market is like. You do not need to be hindered by the limited perceptions of others or by a lack of resources. Discover time-tested principles that will enable you to fulfill your vision no matter who you are or where you come from.

You were not meant for a mundane or mediocre life.
Revive your passion for living, pursue your dream,
discover your vision—and find your true life.

ISBN: 978-0-88368-951-6 • Hardcover • 240 pages

www.whitakerhouse.com